PREFACE

This book is a reprint of an untrimmed, unbound copy which was found in the effects of the late Harvey A. Donaldson. Apparently at some time it came into the possession of W. Milton Farrow's daughter, since she signed the title page. How Donaldson obtained it is anyone's guess.

We've been unable to learn how many copies were printed but we do know that an original bound edition exists in the Ray Riling Library — one of the most complete gun book collections in the world. From a phone call to the Information Operator in Rhode Island we learned that Davis & Pitmat Printers no longer exists, as was suspected. We called the Copyright Office in Washington, D.C., and confirmed that copyright papers were filed in 1882, but the office clerk could not tell us if the copyright had ever been renewed. She said "apparently not."

You'll see that this is actually two books in one, with *Hints to Beginners* having new chapter numbers. The only change in this reprint from the original is the location of certain drawings or photos. Since these particular pages were not numbered, repositioning was necessary to maintain continuity of page numbers.

We think you'll find this a delightful book and a valuable addition to your library. Farrow was considered the top rifleman of his time, and he was determined to impart his knowledge and experience to others. His keen sense of humor, exemplified in the tales of travels around the world, is a distinct bonus for the reader.

Dave Wolfe

Manufactured in the United States of America
Reprinted July, 1980

ISBN: 0-935632-02-6 Hard Bound
0-935632-03-4 Soft Bound

Wolfe Publishing Co., Inc.

P.O. Box 30-30
Prescott, AZ 86302

HOW I BECAME

A CRACK SHOT,

WITH

HINTS TO BEGINNERS,

By W. MILTON FARROW,

WINNER OF

The ALBERT PRIZE, £100.
The WIMBLEDON CUP, value £100. } England.

SEVRES VASE, by Pres't Grevy,
BRONZE STATUE "VICTORY," by M. le Compte Vendeuvre. }
France.

The CHAMPIONS' MATCH,   '78
The WIMBLEDON CUP MATCH,   '80 } Creedmoor.
The MILITARY CHAMPIONS' MATCH, '82

———•◆•———

NEWPORT:
DAVIS & PITMAN, PRINTERS,
1882.

HOW I BECAME A CRACK SHOT.

Chapter I.

I was born at Belfast, Waldo County, in the State of Maine. My father was a native of Bristol in the same State, and served his country during the war of 1812. It was his misfortune to be for a time confined in the prison at Halifax. My grandfather was a sergeant in one of the companies during the war of the Revolution, and was present at the surrender of Cornwallis. Descended from such stock my claim to be a *thorough* American is certainly a valid one.

From my earliest recollections the love for powder and bullets, rifles and guns, was paramount to balls, tops, marbles, or any of the games of boyhood. Cannons, improvised from tin pen-holders, mounted on blocks with pins, were the first essay. The premature explosion of this weapon with its natural consequences brought disfavor from parental source, and powder was one of the interdicted substances. By a lucky trade with an old junk man a rusty horse-pistol barrel was obtained, mounted on an oak block, secured by an iron staple. It proved a source of great delight. The standing piles on the pier-head, 300 yards' distance, was the enemy, and many were the pounds of lead fired away in the attempt to make " Long Tom " do fine work.

School vacations were spent when possible on board father's vessel, a goodly schooner of seventy tons burthen, plying in the coasting trade from Belfast, east and west; here the use of the shot gun was learned and chances for practicing on coots and ducks were never neglected. The feelings of triumph were most keenly enjoyed when returning to the vessel in harbor from some neighboring ledge of rocks or island in the bay with a goodly bag, to hear the hearty praises from older lips. Never will I forget my first bag of that most wily bird, the "Black Duck" of the coast. One November morning I noticed with the telescope a flock of ducks feeding over the bar running from Tory's to Trumpet Island in Eggemoggin Reach, a sinuous passage amongst the islands, running east and west on the coast of Maine. The schooner was in Centre Harbor. I informed father of the ducks in sight and I desired to go after them. Smiling and shaking his head, he replied: "Black ducks! you want to go after black ducks, it takes an older hunter than you are to shoot black ducks." I at last got his consent to try. After stepping the mast in the boat alongside and the gun passed in I pushed off. A light southerly breeze soon carried the boat out into the Reach. Yes, the ducks were still there. Steering for the leeward point of Tory's Island, my plan was formed to land on the side opposite the birds and try to stalk them through the grass. Gun in hand I stepped on the outer shore of the island to walk towards the farther point where the birds were feeding. The high bank would conceal my approach up to one hundred yards, then the grass was barely high enough to conceal one lying flat. The gun I carried as I took my way along was an old muzzle-loading twelve bore which was in the usual condition of guns kept on ship-board, barrels like a rusty bar, the locks inclined to be weak, and the hammers rather shaky, but for all that it had a reputation for killing coots and ducks second to none in the county. My progress through the grass was very slow as I pushed the gun in advance. I had received minute instructions from father never to get in front of the gun in crawling or working my way up to birds, as it was better to occasionally lose a shot than to run the risk of shooting myself drawing the gun towards me by the muzzle. The grass was getting thin in front. I must be near the bank on the side next the ducks. With both hammers at full cock I raised nearly up, my left elbow still on the ground. Thirty yards in front were the ducks, a flock of fifteen or more. Aiming for the centre of the bunch I pulled the trigger; a sharp click was the only response, but every duck's head was straight up at the sound. Nervously my finger felt for the left-hand trigger, when *bang* went the other barrel, without any aim, up went the ducks as only "blackies" can "go up" not a feather touched. I could have cried, as I lay and watched their receding forms. Presently I noticed they had changed their course, were swinging toward me with intent to cross the bar between the islands, but the strong southwest wind blows them leeward fast, they are flying at right angles to the wind and will cross within shot. I feel for another "G. D.," but the box of caps was left in the boat. On come the ducks. I sit up now and look at them, sixty, forty, only thirty yards away, and bunched so beautifully.

I put up the old crow-bar as I had called it, to show what I could have done had I not forgotten the caps and derisively pulled the trigger right at the middle of the flock.

Bang!—I was nearly laid flat. Enough of the fulminate from the "G. D." cap had remained on the cone to cause the explosion of the powder. Jumping to my feet I looked for the birds. The aim was deadly. Five of them dropped on the point and the shore, two others left the bunch and after a moment set their wings and slowly settled to the waters of the Reach. My joy knew no bounds. How I caressed and patted the rusty barrel which the moment before I had so feelingly dubbed a crow-bar. I picked up my ducks, three with broken wings and two killed outright, put them in the boat and started in the direction I had marked the two crippled ones. One only I found floating dead, then headed the boat for the harbor. I carefully concealed the ducks under the stern sheets and ranged alongside. "Pity the ducks were so shy. Hand up the gun. I was watching through the glass when you fired. How near did you get to them?" "About thirty yards," I replied. "Thirty yards and not drop one! Well, well, I expected better work

than that after all my instructions; what
was the matter?" "Oh, the gun missed
fire and I pulled off the second barrel without taking aim." "I thought I heard you
shoot a second time. What did you fire
at?" with a little impatience. "Come,
jump up out of that boat." Coming to the
side of the vessel just as I pulled out one
duck he said, "What have you got there?"
"Where?" I answered, as I tried to conceal the bird behind me. "A black duck?"
inquiringly and with some astonishment.
"Yes," I shouted, "and another and
another," I repeated, until I had tossed on
the deck the six beautiful birds. My triumph was complete, and boy like, I
shouted, "Now I guess you will think I
can shoot black ducks as well as some older
hunters." I cannot describe his astonished
looks. He had seen the ducks fly away
uninjured, and then to have them introduced so suddenly to his attention was too
much for his equilibrium. "Well done,
well done!" "Six." "Why—how—how
—did—you—do—it?" and he looked at

the ducks then at me two or three times.
A full explanation followed with congratulations encore. I remember at the next
meal, however, the favors of kind Providence were mentioned most devoutly in the
Grace.

ᴇʀ II.

a life on the water it
ton must learn a trade
llege." I was allowed
fortunate circumstance
ᴏꜰ ʟᴀ... s watch to the jewelers,
decided the question. I was apprenticed
to Hiram Chace for three years to learn the
watch making and jewelry business, and
here I may say that this early practicing at
such fine work, which so much depended
upon the steadiness of the hand and nerve,
no doubt laid the foundation for that command of nerve and will power that,
especially in off-hand target shooting, is so
necessary for success. It was promised on
father's part, if I gave a good account of
myself at the end of the three years, he
would give me as my own the " Red, White
and Blue," a small three sail yacht, which
for beauty and speed, in my eye, far sur-

passed any of the other boats to be found in
Belfast Bay.   After three years steady
application to this business and finding my
health somewhat impaired, I decided to go
down among the islands in my own yacht,
camping, hunting and fishing, and thus
enjoy a vacation that I sadly felt in need of.
Enlisting a friend about my own age for the
expedition, we made our preparations.   I
furnished a double barrel shot gun, he a
small muzzle loading rifle, and with plenty
of provisions, we started down Penobscot
Bay. Passing Long Island on the starboard
hand, we turn to the eastward by Cape
Rosier and enter Eggemoggin Reach,
which extends from Pumpkin Island to the
south and east, nearly to Mt. Desert, our
objective point.   Innumerable were the
shots we had at the divers, coots and gulls.
The end of the first week found us at
anchor near Ship Island, where we proposed to stop a few days, and try to capture
a seal, as we had seen a number around
the ledges to the southward of the Island,
and the fishing also was very fine in that

vicinity. The next morning found us on
our course for the fishing ground. We
arrived in season to take advantage of the
slack tide, and secured a goodly number of
cod and pollock. This was George's first
experience with the latter fish, and the first
that he hooked was a lively one. "Oh, I've
got him, I've got him," he repeated. And
it really seemed so, for he was pulling in
the line very fast. "What is it?" I inquired.
An expert fisherman can tell the kind that
has been hooked long before the fish breaks
water. I had barely put the interrogatory
when, "Snub! Snub!" His line suddenly
stopped. He could not budge it. "Look
out!" I cried. The warning came too late,
the line had begun to Zip! Zip! through
his fingers, and the fish now having got
head downward, made the line "sing"
through his hands so fast it seemed like a
red hot wire, and he let go, crying, "Oh!
oh! I'm burnt, I'm burnt." "Catch the
line," I cried," you will lose the fish." "To
h——l with the fish, oh! oh!" and he
rubbed his hands and bemoaned his luck in

such accents of genuine feeling, I was con-
strained to examine them ; but I could not
see that line go overboard entirely, and I
jumped forward just in time to catch the
reel or frame, upon which the cod lines are
generally wound, as it was going over the
side.   The hold I made on it, with the sudden stopping, turned the fish, and I began
to haul in as fast as I could ; five fathoms
came in,—ten fathoms, when, snub ! snub !
but I was prepared for it, and with a dex-
terous turn round the end of a cleat I held
on.   Once more I began to pull in.   George
had forgotten his burning hands in the excitement now, and stood ready to help me.
" Get that gaff and be ready to hook him,"
I shouted.   What a beautiful telephone that
line must have been.   I had no sooner spoken
than the fish redoubled his efforts to get
head down again, and this time with success, but I did not hold the line so tight as
to burn my fingers, and after the fish had
run nearly to the bottom, I thought it was
my turn to " snub ! snub !" which I did,
and I soon had the pollock heading up

again. His efforts to stop were not so frequent now, becoming evidently fatigued or
conquered. I brought him to the surface
and George with the gaff at once lifted him
out, a ten pound pollock. "That's what I
call a lively fish," he cried, "I didn't expect
any such fishing as this." "How are your
hands," I answered. "All right now, here
goes for another of the same sort," and he
threw over his hooks freshly baited. With
the admonition to make the end of his line
fast, I left him to try my own.

We soon had all the fish we wanted and
I suggested we should go up near the
Barge and Jolly Boat Ledges to look for
seals. It was a long way to windward
from Placentia Head to the ledges, but we
made it in good time. The tide had risen
some but still I detected with the aid of the
spy-glass a number of seal on the rocks;
with rifle and gun ready we gradually
approach; we sail up to within one hundred yards of the rocks, I dare not go
nearer with the yacht. "Get ready, George,"
I almost whispered, and give it to that

middle one. I fancied he would be more likely to hit some of them if he fired at the one in the centre. We heard the bullet sing as it bounded from the rock, and the way the seals bounded, too, one would almost imagine they had wings. In a second, almost, not a seal was in sight except the head of one or two a long distance away in the water. "I put some life into them, anyhow," said George. "Yes," I replied, "but see, there is one right ahead, you take the helm, it is my turn to shoot," and I took the shot-gun and ran forward. Keep her off a little, I motioned, steady. At about thirty yards I fired. The gun was loaded with No. 6 shot and as the boat was bouncing about some, I had to take a quick aim. A clean miss was the result, but the sprinkling of the shot or the noise of the gun caused the seal to turn towards us before going down. We were then at about twenty yards distance when I fired the second barrel right in his face. "He is hit, he is hit, see the water fly!" ejaculated George. As we sail over the

place I see the water is tinged with blood.
After "lying to" for a long while and seeing no signs we start for our anchorage.
"I am not satisfied," remarked my companion, "I think you killed that seal. I
will take the dingy and row down there."
"Oh! nonsense," said I. "Seals always
sink when killed, and in deep water it is
seldom they are captured." "Let's go
down, anyhow." He was so anxious I
consented. Placing a flounder spear in the
boat, with gun and rifle we, started. It was
two miles at least to the ledges, but the
wind being with us we soon made the distance. Carefully we rowed round the largest
of the ledges, near the place where the seal
went down. When on the opposite side of
the rocks we noticed a roundish point projecting from the water. "That's him,"
whispers George. "Take the rifle this
time." Carefully taking aim, I fire. The
water splashes just by his nose, and as the
seal goes down in a cloud of spray I cannot
tell if I hit or no. We row round and
round the ledge, but no sign of our game.

As we were about to give up I fancied I saw something floating near where the seal last went down. We carefully row up and I take the spear and stand in the bow of the little boat as we silently approach. Ten feet, now six feet only divide us; three feet, and with all my force I drive the spear through the neck of a baby seal that is so fat he could not stay down. I had obliterated his eye-sight with the shot-gun, he could not see where to go, and so much fat acted as a float and brought him to the surface. His struggles were fierce and it seemed for a moment that we were in danger of being upset, as I tried to lift him with the spear into the boat. I saw the danger and held him away. The spear had passed through the fleshy part of the neck and was secure, still he lashed the water into foam and threw the spray completely over us. Finding a convenient piece of drift-wood in the boat I draw up to the seal, now becoming somewhat exhausted, and a succession of rapid blows on the head and nose takes his life at once.

We haul in our trophy and find a young seal of about three months' growth, which explains the fact of our getting so near to him in the morning. It was a long pull back to the yacht, but the fact of our success lightened the labor and we noted not the time.

Thus we passed nearly three weeks, and after capturing another seal and catching fish to our hearts' content, we left for home. In September I started on another trip, but the disastrous gale of the 15th of that month wrecked my yacht and cast me ashore upon the rocks. We returned home by land and it was then I found I must enter upon the stern realities of life. No more play. I must devote my time to business. My three years' stay at the jewelry trade had fitted me to earn my own livelihood, and with a first class recommendation from my late employer I started for Boston, where I soon found a situation quite to my liking.

Chapter III.

The following Spring I came to Newport, R. I., where after four years' sojourn
I opened business for myself. The Centennial year, the visit of the Foreign Team
at Creedmoor and the publication of their
scores first drew my attention to rifle shooting. One day, after reading the scores of
the Americans, I said to brother, who
was with me in my business, "I believe I
can shoot a rifle as well as some of those
gentlemen." He at once replied: "Why
don't you try?" I sent at once and purchased a first class long range rifle, and
began practice at 200 and 500 yards. My
labors at the watch bench in holding and
fixing the tiny parts of the movements no
doubt contributed in a great measure to the
education of my nerves for the holding and
sustaining at a fine point, the aim upon
the bull's eye. The adjustment of the "rear

sight" and "wind gauge," for the corrections of the elevation and the deviations of
the bullet by the wind, were difficulties
that were quickly surmounted and I began
to shoot well from the very start. In a
short time a rifle club was formed of which
I soon became the leading marksman.
My first medal was won in the club. It
was given for ten shots at 200 yards ; to be
won three times before becoming the personal property of the winner. This prize
was captured in three out of the only four
competitions.

I made a study of projectiles, the velocity of the wind, and the radiation of light
and heat, in order to find their bearing and
influence upon the practice of the art.

The first match entered into at the long
ranges, 800, 900 and 1000 yards, was shot
at Blackstone Range, near Providence, R.
I., October 4th, 1876. It was the "Fall
Shoot" of the local rifle organization at that
place. The prize was a new "magazine"
pistol to be competed for with seven shots
at each distance. It was my second attempt

in scoring at these extreme ranges, but meeting with good success in finding the "bull's eye" at the first stage of the shooting, I was lucky enough to carry off the prize with a score of 86 out of a possible 105, which for the day and those times was considered to be first class work. Some prominent shooters were at this meeting and took part in this very match, and among them were Messrs. N. Washburn, F. J. Rabbeth and George Davidson and many others, who had made local reputations upon this range.

My next essay with the rifle was at Saratoga, on the way to the Centennial. I took my gun along and went up the river to attend a small meeting. At that meet I took the second prize, at 600 yards, with a score of 46 out of a possible 50, and first prize at the 200 yards with a score of 44.

In the Spring of 1877, I went to New York to learn the rifle business, and secured a situation with the agents for the manufacture of the "Ballard Rifle."

My first season at Creedmoor I had much

to learn, being brought into open competition with the crack shots of the country. I found a little sharper practice than I had before seen, but met with some success, especially in one match, at the long ranges, by the Amateur Rifle Club, of which I had become a member, for a bronze medal which was presented by the National Rifle Association, to be competed for with 15 shots at the distances of 800, 900 and 1000 yards. The competition was a very spirited one, such shots as I. Allen, H. Jewel, N. Washburn and other members of the club took part. The score was 203, out of a possible 225, which was considered a very creditable one, under the circumstances. I also made my first winning for the "Turf, Field and Farm" Challenge Badge, a medal that must be won three times before it could become the personal property of the winner.

CHAPTER IV.

In the Winter of 1878 I went to California on a business trip, and in April of that year won a medal against all comers, shooting 60 shots at 200 yards, on a ring target, ¾ inch rings. The prize was a beautiful medal given by the San Francisco Turnverein Society at Alameda Park. The score was 1,268 rings, leading by 100 points the next best competitor.

NOTE.—We here condense a portion of Mr. Farrow's narrative which relates to a somewhat unpleasant experience abroad. The facts being fairly stated the reader can form his own opinion as to his treatment. —[Ed.

Mr. Farrow returned to New York to compete in the grand festival of the Sharpshooters' Union of America, held in the following June at Union Hill, New Jersey, where he won the King's Medal, and on the Target of Honor a splendid silver

600 shots, 200 yards, off-hand.
Score 1049 points.

Hits in 12 in. black only to count.
Scoring 1, 2 and 3.

champagne cooler. His score was 1,049 points, and he was crowned as the Schutzen King, to reign until the next festival which was to take place in three years from that time.

Immediately after the Schutzen Fest, Mr. Farrow sailed for Europe and appeared for the first time among the sportsmen of Wimbledon. Here he won a number of prizes and then went to Dusseldorf, where he won several medals and a silver cup. His reception there by the local marksmen was not so cordial as he expected, from the position he occupied with the Germans in America, representing as he did the German shooting clubs. Having been crowned king of all the shooters in the United States of that style of shooting, he naturally expected a friendly reception at least. The manner of shooting in Germany was somewhat different from that practiced in America. Guns of only about thirteen pounds weight being allowed and also "open sights" or sights that could be construed to be open, might be used; while on this side of the water, guns of any weight, with "peep" and "globe sights," were allowable for competition. After the modification of the sights, then the knack of proper holding and the adjustment of the elevations was something that one must become accustomed to. With these disadvantages it was hardly to be expected that any of the local shooters at Dusseldorf would be jealous of the efforts of the representative shots coming from such a distance; but when Mr. Farrow went to shoot on the Target of Honor, this competition consisted of two shots only on the Ring Target; the first attempt was rewarded with a nineteen, twenty being the dead centre, the highest possible to be made with one bullet. When coming out of the shooting stand one of the shooting masters, named Decker, seized his rifle from his hand with some imprecation muttered in German, and began a violent harangue in that language, which being translated by a friend was to the effect that some one had complained that Mr. Farrow's rifle was too heavy, and infringed the rules in other respects. All rifles brought into the competition, according to the rules, have to pass through the hands of an examining committee who attach a seal to the guns showing that they have been examined and approved by their hands. Upon exhibiting the seal to the shooting master, his reply was, he "*didn't care a damn for the seals, he would examine the gun for himself.*" Mr. Farrow suggested to him that out of courtesy, at least, he should allow him to finish his score which he had already begun, but Decker would not surrender the gun and marched off with it in his possession. His object, undoubtedly, was to upset or agitate the shooter that his next shot would be anything but a "bull's eye," as a shot of that description would give to the American the grand silver urn presented by Kaiser William. Upon his return with the rifle Mr. Farrow, through his interpreter, informed the shooting master, who he was, exhibited his King's Medal of the United States, and asked the German if he supposed, that coming from such a distance and representing such a class of men, he would try to win by fraud? The German's reply may have been characteristic, anyway it was very emphatic, "*He didn't care a damn for Mr. Farrow or his medal either.*"

The excitement consequent upon such an interruption was enough to shake the steadiest nerves, and such outrageous treatment, where something more gentle was expected, was too much for the American. The next shot was not a bull's eye but near to it, though far enough away to accomplish the object Mr. Decker had in view. Another American was treated in almost exactly a similar way, which would go to show that the whole thing was a premeditated affair.

From Dusseldorf he journeyed to Stuttgart. His reception there by the riflemen of that club was very cordial, Mr. Edward Foehr, the President of the Association, tendering all the civilities and extending the use of the shooting house and grounds for a friendly competition; indeed, such was the kindness of this gentleman, that it was in his society and at his invitation, that Mr. Farrow visited the Palace of King Charles of Wurtemburg its art galleries and floral conservatories, and to all the other principal attractions of the city he was personally conducted.

From Stuttgart to Friedericksharphen, across Lake Constance, by rail to Waldshutt.

The Swiss are limited to use their government cartridge, which is of a "rim-fire" description, with a bullet of 42 calibre. None of Mr. Farrow's rifles being able to take this ammunition, they were of course debarred from any competition.

From Waldshutt to Schaffhausen, and then to Basle, from Basle to Paris where the French Exposition was in progress, here a study of the Ordnance Department was an interesting subject to which considerable time was devoted.

At this point it might be well to remark that to travel in foreign countries for any particular object, either of sport or the introduction of business, it is Mr. Farrow's opinion that one must make one trip in order to know how to go another time. So this first experience on the other side gave so much information and so many points that the after successes were no doubt due to the knowledge gained in this journey.

Champions Match.
1878.

CHAPTER V.

Mr. Farrow returned from abroad just in time to take part in the meeting of the National Rifle Association at Creedmoor in 1878. Here the championship match was the highest prize. It included the grand gold medal of the Association which was the "Blue Ribbon" of the meeting. The highest honor to be obtained in the Fall meeting, was to win this championship match; it consisted of ten shots each, at 200, 600 and 1000 yards. Mr. Farrow started in at the 200 with a score of 46, at the 600 yards 47 points, and at the 1000 yards 46, making a total of 139, which was four points ahead of any other competitor. Thus it may be seen that in two years time, Mr. Farrow had risen to the position of *champion rifle shot of the United States*. This match is a yearly competition at Creedmoor. It is open to all comers and the valuable prize given by the N. R. A. is well worth the competing for.   This closed the shooting season of 1878.

The monthly meetings of the National Rifle Association for the year 1879 began on April 16th with the fifteenth competition for the Challenge Badge, presented by the "Turf, Field and Farm." The conditions of this match called for 10 shots at 200 yards, "off-hand," the medal to be won three times before becoming the personal property of the winner.

This fifteenth competition proved to be the last, having won it on two previous occasions with the scores of 42 and 44.   I was again a winner with a higher score than had yet been made during the 14 previous competitions, 47 out of a possible 50.

And here I will remark that the value of these competitions, at 200 yards off-hand, to any marksman, is much underrated by the average range officer at Creedmoor. There is no point in rifle shooting that will test a man's steadiness of nerve and his

Given by Turf, Field & Farm.
Creedmoor, 200 yards, off-hand.
Won 3 times.

reliability as a competent marksman to put on a team, than this 200 yard off-hand shooting. The person who can or does become a strong off-hand shot, can overcome all the obstacles in shooting at any other range or distance, and I will also say, that the old adage, "It is a poor rule that won't work both ways," may, in this case, be considered a poor rule, for it will not work in the opposite direction; it is not always, that a first class long range marksman, can become a first class short range or off-hand shooter.

Some weeks prior to the match just related, the Annual Gallery Tournament of "The Forest and Stream" came off at an up town New York gallery. The conditions called for teams of ten men, to shoot 10 shots each on a Creedmoor target reduced for the distance.

There were ten teams entered, in all 100 men. The shooting lasted for five days. The team of which I was a member won first place; the prizes consisted of a gold medal to each member of the winning team. Personally making the best score of the one hundred men, it seems that a slight mention of the circumstance will not be out of place.

The following June sees our marksman again crossing the Atlantic. The golden prizes at Wimbledon and the tempting shoots on the continent, were the attractions which beckoned him to take part.

The annual meetings at Wimbledon of the British National Rifle Association are held generally the second and third weeks in July. At this meeting frequently from ten to twenty thousand pounds are distributed as prizes amongst the competing marksmen. A great many of the matches are open to all comers, and the prizes are liberal and attractive. Many of these matches are arranged to admit sporting guns of American pattern, and to these matches most of our attention was directed; the particular one being the "Albert" prize which consisted, in 1879, of two stages; the first stage was 200, 600 and 900 yards, and only the winners of a prize in this first competition are allowed to compete in the second stage of the match, which was 15

Prize Certificate
National Rifle Association
Wimbledon.

1879

100 { 2nd Stage. Albert". 15 Shots 1000 Yds.
      { Score 70 Marks. (Ballard Rifle.)

Won By

Private W. Milton Farrow.
Newport R.I. Art". U.S.A.

"Albert," £100, England.

shots at 1000 yards : there being in this stage one prize only, one hundred pounds cash.

The prize in this match was originally given by Prince Albert before his demise, and has been perpetuated by the Association in remembrance. It is considered the greatest honor to win this match next to the Queen's prize, which was not open to any Americans.

With a score of 70 points out of a possible 75, our champion takes away the one hundred pounds, the first time it was ever won by any American. At this meeting Mr. Farrow also made 34 in the " Alfred " match, out of a possible 35, and in the St. Leger, making the highest possible score, *all bulls' eyes* in a possible 35, also making 33 in a possible 35 of the extra *third series*, another 34 out of a possible 35 in the Graphic, which was 7 shots at 1000 yards.

This series of matches were open to all comers and the competitions were fairly and honorably contested; indeed, the system of the competitions, the scoring and

the marking as carried on at Wimbledon
is among the fairest and most perfect of
any rifle association in the world.

The Albert prize was personally presented to Mr. Farrow by the Duchess of
Connaught as was also the St. Leger.

The shoot at Versailles followed close
upon the Wimbledon meet. On arriving
in Paris with a letter of introduction to a
prominent member of the society there,
Mr. Farrow was advised by this gentleman
to take a trip to Caen in Normandy. An
international shoot was in progress at that
place for some valuable prizes, notable
among which was a Sevres china vase
presented by President Grevy, also a
bronze statue given by "M. le General
Count de Vendeuvre depute du Calvados,"
also the "Tromp-de-Ury," which consisted
of an immense horn fitted up with nickel
trimmings ; following the crook on the
outside from base to point it is 3 feet, 10
inches in length and about 18 inches around
the base,—a most valuable trophy, very
rare and unique. Taking but 100 rounds

of ammunition with his rifle, an immediate start was made on that Friday—from the fact that the shoot would close the following Monday. With no letters of introduction, with no personal acquaintance and no friendly notice from any one, he landed in Caen with barely sufficient knowledge of the French language to get along in a restaurant. It seemed like attempting a forlorn hope to enter a competition for these prizes, but trusting to find a "fair field and no favor" the American shooter was determined to at least shoot his way or push his way by fair marksmanship to the attention of the competitors at the meet; but the events that followed here are best given in Mr. Farrow's own language.

I landed at the English Hotel, where they were supposed to speak English, some one, but the broken English that was spoken by the proprietor was something horrible. It was impossible, almost, to make one's self understood or to understand him, but after a somewhat protracted conversation, I gave him to understand I wished to take part in

the rifle shoot, and he directed me to a gun
store that was kept near—by one of the
active members of the club, who, when I
called there, introduced me to the Secretary
of the Association, a gentleman that had
seen some service in England and could
manage to speak considerable English.
With him I got along very nicely and we
started for the rifle range of 200 metres,
which was situated at Cruelly, some half a
mile from the city.   Knowing that there
was a radical difference between 200 metres
and 200 yards, for which my sights were
arranged, it required a change in the elevation to correct for the difference.   I knew
a metre was practically one-tenth longer
than a yard.   I adjusted my sights for what
would be about 220 yards, and procured a
ticket of entrance to the match for the prize
given by the President.   This match consisted of six shots at 200 metres, off-hand.
On my first attempt I found the elevation
calculated was a trifle too high, and the bullet landed in the ring which counts 4, just
above the bull's eye; the next five succes-

sive shots the bullets were fairly planted inside the bull's eye, making a score of 29 in a possible 30. The Secretary, upon the conclusion of the score, enthusiastically patted me on the back and exclaimed, "You have won ze prize given by President Grevy." I was somewhat astonished at the fact, as the shooting was upon conditions which appeared quite easy to me, and I expected at least that during the three weeks that the shoot had been in progress a full score had probably been made. I then fired a few shots with their military rifle, wishing to inform myself of the range and accuracy from a personal inspection. The rifle was a Chassepot; the ammunition appeared to be loaded with a paper patch bullet, and then lubricated with a thick covering of grease or tallow, which, in my mind, explains the fault of extreme inaccuracy of the rifles. Being satisfied with the experiment, I returned to my own rifle, and wishing to show the gentlemen that the shooting I had just made was not the result of accident, I procured another ticket in this match and succeeded in making another score of 29 in a possible 30.

The enthusiasm of the Secretary at this feat was unbounded. He wished to know my standing and all the particulars of my voyage and trip, and upon our return to the city at 12 o'clock, the shooting having ceased, he immediately proclaimed the intelligence to the members of the club and his friends of the extraordinary feat of the American marksman.

Chapter VI.

In the afternoon, from one P. M., the shooting was continued at the 170 metres range, which was situated in the city. The ruins of an old castle were there and the range was located in the moat. The high walls on each side afforded ample protection from the wind. and the shooting being from indoors, the conditions were very favorable for fine scores. The target at this 170 metres was of a different character from the one used at the 200 metres. The lines were drawn finer or closer. The bull's eye, which was 4 inches in diameter, counted 10, the next ring was 9, the next 8, and so out to the unit.

The principal match here, was for the bronze statue already mentioned, which trial consisted of six shots, the highest possible score being 60 points. Not knowing what had already been scored I procured a ticket and on the first six shots secured a total of 54. The Secretary then informed me that 55 was the highest figure yet reached by any marksman, and that only by M. de St. Paul. As I was finishing my second score, this being a re-entry match, I noticed near the entrance of the shooting house some ladies, and in fact upon looking around I perceived that the shooting house was very nearly filled with marksmen and spectators who were watching the progress of the match, making many remarks, with animated gestures, which conveyed the impression to my mind, that as I was the only one competing at the time, they were discussing the relative merits of the score. The atmosphere being very close I tried to procure a glass of water, but was informed that it could not be had, it was not on the premises. If I had asked for ale or wine or beer or spirits of any kind, it would have been forthcoming immediately, but a glass of water for a shooter was something not heard of in that country. I was then introduced by the

Secretary to Madam de Saville and her two sons, one of whom had been educated in England and could speak English quite fluently. He explained to me that his mother had been informed of the scores at the Cruelly Range, and had come down to witness my shooting in the match for the bronze figure. I replied that I was very much honored by their presence, that it sometimes happened to marksmen, at the very moment when wishing to do their best, that they became nervous and actually made poorer scores than would ordinarily be the case, but I would do my utmost to please them; explaining to him I desired a glass of water, the atmosphere being very close. He told one of the soldiers of my wishes and then sent him out to a neighboring house and procured a supply. The shooting on the other firing points had entirely ceased for the time, and the interest was all centred on the score I was about to make while the ladies were present. Taking my rifle in hand I began a third score, the first bullet of which struck

in the ring next to the bull's eye and
counted 9. Monsieur de Saville, pointing
to a target on the wall, a *fac simile* of the
one I was shooting at, explained to the
ladies where the bullet had struck. Cleaning my rifle, I prepared for the next shot.
This I happily placed in the bull's eye,
counting 10. A murmur of satisfaction
went through the hall as the marker proclaimed the position and value of the shot;
the third shot was also a bull's eye, counting 10. At this the Madam clapped her
hands and in a subdued tone cried,
"Bravo!" "Bravo!" The young gentleman crossed to where I was standing and
remarked to me: "My mother is very
much pleased with your shooting." My
answer was "Tell your mother I can but
shoot well in the presence of ladies." This
pleasing little incident no doubt added
greatly to the good feeling engendered by
the accuracy of the shooting. The 4th
shot was another 9, the 5th shot was again
planted in the bull's eye, and a murmur of
satisfaction went around once more. Now

everything depended upon the last shot, and marksmen who have been placed in the same position I was in at that time will no doubt understand the peculiar situation, and it is only those marksmen who have made a series of fine shots and are reduced to the last on the score to make a *sure win*, who *can* know and understand the nervous strain and consequent intense excitement which is the result of this condition. The slightest tremor of the gun, the least accidental pressure of the finger, ruins every chance. It was while under the influence of these feelings that I raised the rifle for the last shot. A silence equalling that of death fell upon the interested company ; a little nervous tremor I felt and without hesitation rested the gun down upon the shooting bench in front of me. A gentle hum of conversation was indulged in by those behind, the purport of which I well knew. Bracing myself once more I raised the rifle quickly and in an instant fired. At the instant of discharge I cried "*neuf*" (meaning 9), knowing that the bullet had struck inside the ring, calling for 9 points. This indeed was the fact and its verification by the scorer was the signal for an outburst of applause that was as hearty as it was genuine, even the ladies joining in the general enthusiasm. Here was an American marksman whose skill with the rifle was so unprecedented, whose magical scores stopped so little short of the " possible " that the performance seemed bordering on the marvelous. This ended the series of shots upon that ticket, the total of which was 57, giving me two points advantage over any other shooter, thus winning the prize. The young Frenchman once more came to my side and asked me how I knew the last shot was nine points, before the marker or scorer had signaled or indicated the fact. Smiling, I informed him that my rifle always told me at the instant of explosion exactly what the bullet had made. This was something which he could not understand and he had quite an animated ·conversation upon the subject with his mother, she being well posted in rifle matters as her husband was one of the officers of the club and stood well up in the prize list.

After a short rest I was induced to enter the match for the "Tromp-de-Ury" prize, which consisted of a series of sixty shots, 3 cards of 20 shots each. On the first card my total of 20 shots aggregated 182; on the second card the total was the same. Everything went well until my third shot from the last when my bullets were exhausted. I proposed to the Secretary that I should borrow one of their rifles to shoot the remaining three shots. His reply was, "You will lose ze prize." I then suggested that I should not shoot. His reply was the same, "You will lose ze prize." Upon inquiry I found that the rules required each one to shoot his own rifle and to shoot 60 shots consecutively. I must say my ingenuity was somewhat taxed at this point, but a happy idea came to my relief and I asked him to give me three Martini cartridges. I knew there were no cartridges or bullets in all France that were suitable

for my rifle and was forced to do something
rather out of the line ; I removed the bullets
from the Martini cartridges and with my
pocket-knife *whittled* them down to the
size required to fit the calibre of my rifle,
and using some lubrication that I found
there was enabled to finish my score, and
made three close shots and won the prize,
much to the delighted surprise of the Secretary, who had been my best friend from
the start and could hardly understand how
such precision could be obtained from
" *whittled lumps of lead* " as he termed
them.

This ended the shooting for me in Caen.
I found the next day that I had not only
won the three prizes already mentioned,
but the grand gold medal of the society
was also mine, being won by the aggregated scores of the three matches mentioned.

The President and some members of the
society called at the hotel and insisted upon
my staying over a couple of days, as there
would be a public presentation of the prizes
by the Mayor of the city.   After much

persuasion I consented to remain. The prizes were publicly presented in the "Hotel de Ville" by the city notables before a crowded house and a sympathetic audience, for there was such feeling shown that when I stepped forward to receive the vase given by President Grevy, the band struck up Hail Columbia, the audience rose "*en masse*" cheering, with shaking of handkerchiefs and swinging of hats. It was a scene which will long be remembered by me; a single American rifleman in a strange country had so won upon the sympathies and friendship of the entire city that the enthusiasm with which they welcomed him was almost overpowering. It was the grandest and finest public reception in a foreign country that was ever accorded to a single marksman.

After the presentation I was escorted to the balcony where we witnessed a review of the Provencal Corps, and a torch-light procession also filed by with two immense bands playing the "*Marseilles*," in which the people in the streets and in the procession joined, singing it in a very melodious and spirited manner. The evening was otherwise calm and quiet, and the melody of the music from the bands and the voices as it drifted up to the balconies was something most delicious and charming to the ear.

Chapter VII.

My friend in Paris, to whom I soon returned, was very much astonished at my success and remarked to me, " he fancied I would have more difficulty in winning the first prizes at Versailles, as he believed the riflemen there were very proficient," and invited me to appear at the range the following week.

The matches at Versailles were carried on in nearly the same manner as the match at Cruelly, with the exception of the cartons in the bull's eye, which counted six. We were allowed but five shots on each score at Versailles and after my second attempt the shooting appeared comparatively easy. There is a great advantage in a rifleman's becoming accustomed to the range and style of marking and the different manners of scoring. The range at Versailles is situated a short distance from " The Castle " which was built by Napoleon, and many millions of francs were expended upon it and its beautiful surroundings. On entering the shooting grounds one is struck with the cleanliness and pleasant arrangement of the premises, the range, the shooting house, and *cafe* being separated by a plot of ground artistically laid out in flower beds and green sward with gravel walks between. The shooting house is a long building and its arrangement for the convenience of the shooters and spectators is most complete. The different ranges are divided by railings and loading tables for the competitors, and each shooter takes his turn as his name is called by the scorekeeper. The arrangement of the targets is such, that one slides up when the other slides down to facilitate the rapidity of the shooting, so that, as soon as the marksman has fired, he touches a small knob on the right which rings by electricity a bell at the target. The marker in the butts hearing his bell ring, examines the target, marks the shot, and then the value of it is telegraphed back to the shooting house by an arrangement of keys with numbers on them; these numbers are on small discs which, when their key is touched at the target, assume an upright position and show the number to the score-keeper, to the spectators and to the shooter himself; standing upright for an instant it then drops back and remains from sight until re-touched again from the effects of another shot. Nothing could be more convenient in its arrangement to show the spectators and the shooter the value of a shot in so speedy a manner.

At the 200 metres I made two full scores, 30 points each, in a possible 30 points; at the 300 metres I took first prize with 28 in a possible 30 points; at the 150 metres I won first prize with 29 in a possible 30 points.

Here again the American was victorious, winning first prize on every target. I received the most profuse congratulations from my friend, who was now convinced that even the Versailles marksmen were no match for my skill. Soon after leaving

Paris I sailed for the United States, where I again took part in the Fall matches of the National Rifle Association of America. This meeting following so closely my arrival home. I had not recovered sufficiently from the effects of my trip across the Atlantic, to take a very prominent part.

Chapter VIII.

In January, 1880, Mr. Farrow arranged a friendly meeting with the members of the Empire Rifle Club, and the Walnut Hill Rifle Association near Boston. An "everybody's match" was in progress at the time and the New York club anticipated an enjoyable day's sport with their Boston friends. The day proved anything but fine for off-hand shooting, the wind blowing quite a gale and heavy dark clouds rushing across the range, casting their shadows over the targets in a very perplexing manner. Notwithstanding these drawbacks the gentlemen of the Empire Club succeeded in making some good records, Mr. Farrow fairly outdoing himself on this day, making a score that was unprecedented at this distance. We copy a paragraph from the "Boston Globe" in reference to the shooting.

"Five to seven points of wind were used by the gentlemen, consequently, constant watching of windage and elevation was required. Mr. Farrow succeeded in making the most wonderful score on record; after making a full score of 50 points, which has never been done before in a match except by himself at Creedmoor, in November last, he continued his shooting and scored 15 consecutive bulls' eyes, a total of 75, never before achieved by any rifleman in the world, and placing him positively as the King of all marksmen."

The Spring of this year was rather a busy one for the National Rifle Association. The choice of the team to visit Ireland to once more compete against the chosen members of the Irish Rifle Association at Dollymount, and, if possible, win another victory on foreign grounds, engaged their attention.

The N. R. A., in a printed circular, promised to pay the expenses of three men whom they would nominate for the final competitions, provided the nominees retained their places on the team, up to the amount of $350 each. This liberal offer proved quite tempting to a number of marksmen, and a spirited contest took place among the interested ones, the result of which was that Mr. W. M. Farrow was one of the nominated shooters by the N. R. A. and entered the competition for the final selection of men to go across the water. In the shooting off for places, with two scores only to count, Mr. Farrow wins second place, with a total of 216 and 208 respectively.

The voyage across the Atlantic on the steamer was nothing new to him, and on landing at Queenstown his physical condition was in no wise impaired; which was the case with some other members of the team, and good scores from the very start, came as if by magic from the muzzle of his rifle, which scores were happily sustained by him to the very end. Many fine scores were made by the members of the team during the practice at Dollymount before the actual match; for himself Mr. Farrow's score-book shows 216 on two differ-

ent occasions.   This last total will be found
to vary two points, from the total that was
telegraphed across from Dollymount, as the
result of the last practice of the chosen six
men, before the international match took
place.   For some reason, known perhaps
to those in charge of the team, a rather
"smart showing" was given to the reporters
in certain of the scores on that last practice
day.   The result of the match may be
some justification of the irregularity, but
the writer of this volume condemns such
practices in unqualified terms.

The members of the team will long
remember the courtesies and attentions that
were showered upon them, on this visit to
the Land of the Shamrock; their invitation
to Trinity College and dining with the
fellows of that memorable pile, their reception by the Lord Lieutenant of Ireland in
his dining hall, and also the banquet given
by the Lord Mayor of Dublin, the enter-
tainment provided for them by the American Consul; even the boxes at the Opera
House and other places of amusement were

freely opened to the members of the team.

The quarters of the team at the Shelburne Hotel were of the very best description, but the riflemen nominated by the N R. A. which had promised them their expenses to the amount of $350, found the $100, which *only* was given to them, but a drop in the bucket. The $100 was soon exhausted by the very high charges of that hostelry.

This fact of receiving but $100, where $350 was promised, was the occasion of a number of animated discussions among those interested in the matter, and was severely commented upon even by members of the team who were in no way benefitted by their membership. A standing joke at the table of the team was the fact that the bill of fare for dinner, in this Irish hotel, was printed in French and the waiters also were *French* (!) or at least they attempted the accent of the Frenchman in their endeavors to serve the company. If the bill of fare had been printed in *Old Irish* with the greatest amount of brogue and blarney, it was voted by the team 'twould have been more appropriate.

After the conclusion of the international match, the Irish Rifle Association had their annual competition for prizes, mostly open to all comers, but at different ranges and under different conditions; among which was the competition for the " Spencer cup " and several other prizes. The conditions were 10 shots at 800 yards.

Mr. Farrow and Mr. Milner, of the Irish Rifle Association, making 49 each of the possible 50, their scores being an exact tie, were obliged to shoot off, in a series of consecutive shots over the same range. The prize was a beautiful silver biscuit cup presented by Mr. Johnson, of Dublin.

Mr. Milner's first shot was a bull's eye. Mr. Farrow also followed with one, and so it ran up to the fifth shot. The attention of the spectators being called to this fact, the excitement was very keen. Mr. Farrow's 5th was a good " bull." Mr. Milner laid down mid some excitement, but through some inadvertence in pulling or variation of the wind the red disc showed up as the result of his shot, thus giving the cup to his opponent.

Chapter IX.

The annual meeting of the British National Rifle Association at Wimbledon followed soon after the international match with the Irish, and the team, with some exceptions, proceeded there to join in the competitions. Part of them following the advice of old *habitues* of the range procured from the Association the loan of tents and camped on the ground. There are a number of advantages in so doing, and it proved in this case no exception to the rule; as the winners of valuable prizes were those members of the team who camped on the range; while those who lodged in the town, had to take the cabs to the station, then the train to the city, were not in condition upon arriving at the grounds in the morning, to compete with those fresh and "early birds" who had remained all night, and had the

morning to prepare their ammunition, and
perform other small offices that required
their attention.

There are a number of valuable prizes
offered to all comers by the Association
every year.   Among these are prizes which
are open only to certain members of the
Association, for instance, the Wimbledon
cup ; this match consists of fifteen shots at
1000 yards, to those who have won a prize
of at least twenty pounds or more at some
prior meeting of the Association.

Having won the "Albert" prize of one
hundred pounds the year previous, Mr.
Farrow's whole attention was given to the
winning of the Wimbledon cup.   The cup
is a magnificent affair, made by Elkington,
of solid silver and gold.   It consists of a
ewer and salver.   The salver is some 18
inches or more in diameter, with a raised
centre upon which sits a beautiful jug or
ewer of some 12 inches in height, decorated
upon the surface with raised figures of
birds, animals, and human figures with faces
of extreme beauty.   The salver is the handi-

work of an artist, and is in itself, a complete study, bearing as it does in the lower centre mythological pictures of the four elements, and on the raised rim a series of eight pictures, in *bas relief*, of the arts and sciences. The cost of the manufacture of this beautiful prize was one hundred pounds. No prize at Wimbledon is more coveted or sought after than this, as it is impossible to procure a salver and ewer of this pattern in any other way than by winning it at Wimbledon ; the dies, tools and plates used in its manufacture are all controlled by the Rifle Association, and only one cup each year is allowed to be made from them.

We again resume Mr. Farrow's narrative.—[Ed.

After competing in a number of minor matches with some successes, winning second place in the first stage of the Albert competition, with 116 points, and making 34 in a possible 35 at 1000 yards in the Curtis and Harvey match, also taking second and third in the Martin Smith match, I now devoted my whole time and attention to watching the changes and con-

Salver for " Wimbledon Cup,"
England.

Ewer for " Wimbledon Cup,"
England

ditions, and engaging in the pool shooting at 1000 yards, as preparatory practice for this all important match. The competition in this match between the riflemen is so sharp, that the disadvantage of a bad beginning often throws out what otherwise would become a sure winner. There being but one prize, the necessity of starting with a bull's eye is one of the points that needs special attention. The match is called in the morning at 10 o'clock that no pool shooting or previous practice can be indulged in by the contestants and, if possible, that all shall begin under the same conditions as nearly as it can be arranged ; thus showing each one what should delight the heart of every marksman, that is, " a fair field and no favor."

My practice and studies were of the greatest benefit. The first bullet I fired lodged well in the bull, and with the match fairly begun the shots followed on faster and faster   The fluctuations of the wind and light were of such a variable character, the flags upon the range were so badly posted, it was almost impossible to follow with the vernier and wind gauge their changes, with such unerring judgment, but that a skip of the bull's eye was occasionally shown on the target. Up to the 10th or 11th shot I was leading the field by two or three points. A miscalculation of the force of the wind on the next trial resulted in an outer on the right. This gave the other marksmen renewed courage. Luckily for me I captured the bull's eye on the next shot, and with centre and bull then closed the score, having a total of 69 in a possible 75.

Soon after the last shots were fired down the range, it was discovered that Farrow, Evans and Young, each had a total of 69 points. The news of the tie ran through the camp, and when six o'clock was posted as the hour for shooting off the ties, the indications were, that a large crowd would be present to witness the contest. The rules of the Association in this match required that ties *in totals*, should be contested over the same range and decided by the total score of three shots ; if still a tie, then by single shots until the winner is decided.

The afternoon of this day proved anything but an agreeable one. The light was hazy and clouds of smoke rolled up from the city, the wind coming from that direction ; later in the afternoon indications of a drizzle or Scotch mist were present. At 5 o'clock I repaired to the one thousand yard firing point, to engage if possible, in some pool shooting, and secure the elevations and windage that would be necessary to use in the tie shots. I found a subscription match in progress, which I was not aware could be indulged in, with Messrs Evans and Young hard at work showing up bull's eyes and centres with great regularity. The targets by this time were almost totally obscured, and it was by dint of hard labor and close attention that even the scorers could make out the signals of the value of each of the shots as the targets rose and fell.

The targets at Wimbledon are arranged on the window sash principle. The target

proper being in position, a shot is fired, the
marker, seeing the hole that the bullet has left in the target, places upon
the "dummy" target, which is in the pit
before him, a large disc of the proper color
which indicates the value of the shot, in
its approximate position on the target. He
pushes up this dummy when the actual
target drops into the pit, where a
small disc, of some 8 or 10 inches in diameter, is secured upon it by a catch fastened
through the hole made by the bullet. The
target is then run up and the marksman
with his glass or telescope, sees the exact
location of the bullet hole.

I procured a ticket of entrance to this
subscription match that was in progress.
It consisted of 7 shots under the usual conditions. My first two shots were bull's
eyes, then a 4, then a bull's eye, another 4
was shown for my fifth shot. Some
changes in the wind necessitated a slight
alteration of the elevation. Lying down
again, and with careful aim, I fired the 6th
shot. There was no response from the

target. It was a clean miss, but whether the bullet had gone above or below, to the right or left, it was impossible for me to tell. There were but five minutes left before six o'clock, the hour set to begin the shooting off the tie. The news ran along the line "Farrow has made a miss." An anxious feeling went over the American representatives that were watching the shooting and longing for the success of their champion.

With some anxiety I prepared for my final shot. Thinking the matter over as coolly as possible, I decided that the bullet had struck short of the target. Making the necessary corrections of elevation, I proceeded to the firing point and after carefully taking aim, pulled the trigger. All eyes were now turned upon the target, but not a movement was made in that direction. A dozen glasses were brought to bear, but no sign of life was visible. The bull's eye still stood squarely up and seemed as if possessed with no idea of disappearing into the pit. I went back to my seat and sat down to think the matter over.

The drizzle by this time had turned into a veritable shower. Borrowing an umbrella for protection from the wet, I fastened it to the back of a chair and proceeded to clean my rifle. The officer in charge of the match then cried out, "Prepare to shoot off the tie for the Wimbledon cup." I examined my veneer. The elevations appeared all right. I looked again at the conditions; the wind I am sure was at "zero," blowing directly from "six o'clock." I could not have missed that target to the right or left. There was quite six feet on either side of the centre-line of the bull. The fault must be in the elevation. I was either too high or too low, but which? The wind seemed to lull in force, then, I reasoned, "the bullet has dropped short," and I once more raised the veneer and repaired to the firing point. The light, which before the shower was of the worst description, had now become simply miserable; indeed the target could hardly be discerned even with the telescope, and the marking discs as they appeared on the dummy target, were so

indistinct, the contestants intimated to the
officer in charge, that it was impossible to
shoot the tie.   He replied, "My orders are
explicit, the tie must be shot."

The assignment of targets being such
that each one was changed from where our
practice in the subscription match had
placed us, mine being the one on the
extreme right and was so near the edge of
the butt or embankment thrown up behind
the target to stop the bullets, it seemed to
me the most indistinct of them all.

Finding no postponement could be had,
I reclined upon the damp grass for the
opening shot.   It was a long while before
I could discern through the sights a tiny
gray speck, full five-eighths of a mile
away.   With a steady pressure upon the
trigger, I sped the bullet on its flight.
The sergeant who was scoring for this target, glued his eye, as it were, to the telescope.   With a breathless exclamation he
cried, "You are on."   The target had
begun to move ; up rose the dummy with a
slow, majestic movement.   There it stood,

apparently as gray and dusky as the driving rain. No sign of a disc, either black or white, could be discovered with the naked eye. The officer with his field glasses was watching for the signal, and as he could not discover the mark he cried, " What is it?" " What is it?" With a quick movement I turned from the firing point and overhearing his remark, cried, with some feeling, "It is a bull's eye." " So it is, so it is, Farrow 5," was the reply, and the score-keeper put down that magical figure.

Hastily reloading, I moved quickly to the firing point again, anxious to take advantage of the conditions before any change could take place. The red disc rose in response to the second shot, scoring 4. As I retired to my seat to clean the rifle for the last shot, one of my friends whispered, " Evans has closed for 9 points in his total; Major Young has a 5 and a 2 for two shots." I repaired again to the firing point, and not knowing the position upon the target of the 4 I had just made, I could make no calculation or alteration for it. The spotting disc could not be seen even with the most powerful telescope, and the rain seemed to be coming down, if possible, in larger streams. After a long time spent in trying to find the "small gray speck," again I fired; this time the dummy target rose more slowly than before, but the officer discovered the disc marking a 3, called the "Magpie," bringing my total up to 12 points for the three shots. Major Young had yet one shot to fire; if it was landed in the bull's eye he would have another chance, if in any other circle the prize would be mine. The down-pour of rain now nearly ceased, the drops began to come with less force and regularity. I think the major discovered it was lighting up a little, and in a few minutes more a better view of the target would be possible; he seemed favored in this respect as, after lying down and taking a long and careful aim, his gun missed fire, necessitating the retiring again to his ammunition stand and preparing his rifle anew, but with all his care and painstaking a 3 was the responsive signal for his final effort.

Cheers and hearty congratulations were then showered upon America's representative, and both Major Young and Mr. Evans shook hands and warmly congratulated the winner. I may say it was one of the proudest moments of my whole experience; to stand on British soil and be the winner in such a remarkably close and exciting competition, with crowds of spectators of both nationalities watching with interested feelings the entire competition.

Despite the rain and the drizzly weather, I felt light at heart and extremely happy, although wet to the skin and in some danger of taking an influenza.

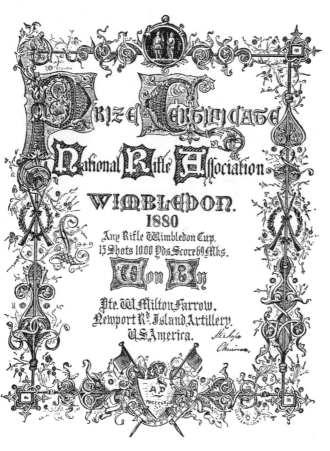

Prize Certificate

National Rifle Association

WIMBLEDON.
1880
Any Rifle Wimbledon Cup.
15 Shots 1000 Yds. Score 69 Mks.

Won By

Pte. W. Milton Farrow.
Newport Rd. Island Artillery.
U.S. America.

From National Rifle Association,
England.

Chapter X.

It was at this meeting an unfortunate affair occurred to which, in a measure, may be attributed the defeat of that scratch team of Americans by the English at Wimbledon. Mr. Farrow was as anxious and as interested to have the match come off successfully as any of the members could well be, from the fact that he knew Sir Henry had anticipated the affair, and desired a competition against the Americans, and had a selected team from the best marksmen England could muster.

We do not think these pages a proper place for the discussion or re-opening of that unpleasant affair, but suffice it to say, it would seem unfortunate that the person who was handling the American marksmen, did not try to heal any dissension that did occur between two members of the team, especially if one of the parties was himself, and some personal benefit to him should accrue from any defection.

Why, on that Saturday morning, did he not go and see Mr. Farrow? A few words with him would undoubtedly have healed the breach, even though his continued postponement of the shooting off the tie, did result in obtaining for him the coveted first prize without the ordeal of shooting the three shots, which the rules of the Association demanded. Mr Farrow actually sacrificed his shooting in the competition with the "any rifle" for the Association cup at 600 yards to please the "gentleman," and went to the team practice at Honuslow. A continued sacrifice of one's self-respect in any measure will become, after a while, a monotonous affair, and so it proved in this case. The last grain to be swallowed was too much, and it resulted in Mr. Farrow's resignation from the team the day before the match.

A notice was posted by the Association that winners of first prizes and prizes of twenty pounds or more could have them presented on the grand stand in the afternoon of the following Saturday. Each winner had to give notice of his intention to be present for the proper arrangement of the programme. It was noised through the camp that the Prince and Princess of Wales would personally present the prizes.

Prize winners were notified to appear at the office of the Association at one o'clock. The line was formed promptly at the hour. A detachment of Highlanders in uniform were acting as a body-guard to the Prince of Wales, and soon after marched to the front of the cottage in which the royal party were taking lunch preparatory to the ordeal of the presentation. It was with great difficulty the police could open a line through the immense crowd to the inside of the enclosure that contained a raised dais, which the winners must ascend to receive their prizes from royal hands.

A sea of heads and faces, closely packed and commingled, some hundred yards in extent, proved a novel sight to several of the winners who for the first time had to appear before such an audience, and they felt no little trepidation as they came forward to receive their prizes. Mr. Farrow was introduced to their Royal Highnesses by Earl Stanhope.

We quote from the London Times : " Mr. Farrow, of the United States, in coming for-forward to receive the " any rifle Wimbledon cup," was introduced to her Royal Highness, the Princess of Wales, by Earl Stanhope."

With hat in hand he ascended the steps to the platform and gracefully bowed at the introduction. As the Princess delivered the valuable plate to his keeping, His Royal Highness remarked, " We congratulate you, Mr. Farrow, upon your success." Thanking the Prince, in reply, for his kindness, Mr. Farrow answered that it was very agreeable to come to Wimbledon and win so valuable a prize, but far more pleasing to receive it from such regal hands.

"Mr. Farrow was loudly cheered as he carried off his handsome prize."—London Graphic.

Mr. Farrow soon after sailed for the United States, arriving in time to make good preparation to attend the Fall meeting of the National Rifle Association at Creedmoor.

The only competitions on the programme for the small bore match rifle were the "Champions" match, ten shots at 200, 600 and 1000 yards, of which Mr. Farrow was the winner in 1878; and the "Wimbledon cup" match, contested for with thirty shots at 1000 yards.

This Wimbledon cup is an immense urn-like affair of solid silver, presented to the American Rifle Association by the British Rifle Association, to be competed for each year at Creedmoor. Thus a winner of the cup could hold it but twelve months, unless he was fortunate enough to make a succeeding winning.

In the Champions match, at the conclusion of the 200 and 600 yards stages, Mr. Farrow was leading by *one point*, all other competitors.

But this year of 1880 was a memorable one, from the fact that there was considera-

ble agitation by certain rifle shots, who
forced their ideas upon the National Rifle
Association, whereby certain members
were to be dubbed "Professionals," and
barred from competition over the "Moor."
A number of these gentlemen were present
and competed in this match, and made a
great deal of fuss and talk. At the 1000
yards range the cry of a certain one was,
"Anything to beat Farrow," and the persecution was carried to such an extent, that
during the necessary arrangement of rifle
and ammunition, to meet the conditions prevailing at this stage of the match, Mr.
Farrow's attention was so diverted from the
prevailing wind and light, he started with
an elevation on his vernier sight some two or
three points too high, and was lucky indeed
to drop into third position in the grand
total, which gave him the bronze medal of
the Association. The wind-up match of
the meeting was for the Wimbledon cup,
and Mr. Farrow's determination to make,
if possible, a win in this match, and his
experiences of the day before with the

marksman referred to, all contributed to strengthen the cool resolve to hold no intercourse with anyone, that might have a tendency to divert his attention, from the actual conditions prevailing during the shooting. The match was called immediately after the lunch hour.   The wind was blowing briskly from the seven to eight o'clock quarter of the range, necessitating an allowance on the wind gauge of from six to seven points.

Starting with a bull's eye, as did but four others out of the twenty-seven competitors in the match, the contest after a few shots had been fired narrowed down to nearly the same gentlemen whose calculations at the beginning were so uniformly verified   The elevations, owing to the increasing velocity of the wind, required careful attention. From an elevation of 206 they were carried down, down to 198¼, still holding the bull's eye with but one or two exceptions in the first fifteen shots ; the wind then began to lull and decreased in force, thus causing an upward turn to the elevations, and before the finish of the thirty shots the vernier readings were 203.

The strength of the wind, as it blew from left to right, was a matter of much importance. It brought many to grief who were unable to detect its variations; the wind allowance on the sight necessitated changes of from two to six points, and as a matter of record which the target here shows, of the thirty shots fired but two of them were outside of the bull's eye, due to mistaken judgment as to the force of the wind. The other three which skipped the charmed circle were owing to changes in the elevations which were not corrected before the shots were fired.

This total of 145 out of a possible 150 stands the highest on record to this day in a match under the same rules.

The news of this score was a surprise to many who had considered Mr. Farrow's abilities limited to the shorter ranges at Creedmoor.

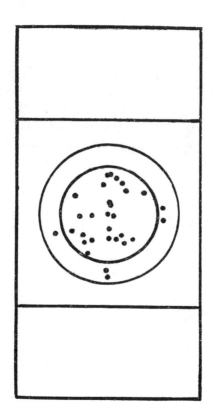

30 shots, 1000 yards. Score 145. Possible 150
Highest on record.
Wimbledon Cup, Creedmoor, 1880.

Chapter XI.

In answer to many pressing invitations from different clubs and societies, Mr. Farrow decided to make a tour to some of the principal cities and, if possible, enliven the interest in rifle shooting.

The first stop was made at Pittsburg, where an interesting shooting was had both at long and short range.

From Pittsburg to Wheeling, West Virginia. This club was entirely an off-hand rifle club and included some very fine shooters. The best record made at this range by Mr. Farrow was three successive scores of ten shots each on the " Massachusetts target," the total of each score being 111, making a grand total of 333 in thirty consecutive shots.

The dimensions of this target are identical with the Creedmoor, with the exception of the addition of lines inside the ordinary three and four rings of the Creed-moor target of 200 yards. The highest count on this "Massachusetts target" is twelve, eleven and twelve being in the eight inch bull's eye, and the circles recede in numbers about two inches apart, out to the "inner" line.

From here Mr. Farrow went to Spring-field, Ohio. There being no rifle club at this place, a meeting was arranged with some of the leading sportsmen and an attempt made to organize one.

Dayton, Ohio, was the next stopping place. There a pleasant incident occurred an account of which we copy from the Journal of that town.

"A Journal reporter was called into Charles E. Schneider's shooting range yes-terday afternoon and requested to shoot with a party of the gunners of this city and a Mr. Bates, a newspaper man from Lima. There was a sly twinkle in Charley Wil-liams' eye as the reporter accepted the invitation, and Charley Schneider hid him-self behind a screen to laugh. There were

five or six men in the contest, and they
banged the bull's eye in a manner that
would have startled Dr. Carver.   Mr.
Bates, strangely for a newspaper man, was
an excellent marksman and rang the little
triangle almost every shot.   Some of the
spectators gazed incredulously, and Charley Williams actually laughed with both
eyes.   After the shoot was over it was
found that Mr. Bates had the best score.
Charley Schneider said the boys had
caught a tartar, and advised them not to
shoot against him.   But they tried another
round with the same result as at first.   The
marksmen scanned the strange arrival from
head to foot and found him to be a medium
sized gentleman, very affable, and with
none of the bluster of a champion.   He
wears a handsome mustache and side
whiskers, and light hair.   Pale, intense,
yet pleasant, he would have been taken for
a calm, shrewd business man, and the last
one in the world for a sportsman.

'Now, gentlemen, allow me to make
you acquainted with Mr. W. M. Farrow,

the champion rifle shot of the world,' said
Mr. Schneider, and then the reporter
opened his eyes. The pleasant, subdued
gentleman was not Mr. Bates, of Lima,
but the same Milton Farrow who had
saved the reputation of the American Rifle
Team at Dollymount, had won more medals
and testimonials for marksmanship than
any other man in the country, and who had
defeated the English, French and Irish on
their own grounds, and according to their
own tactics."

Cincinnati, Louisville, Memphis, St.
Louis, and Springfield, Ill., were each
visited in turn, and many enjoyable meetings were had with the marksmen. At
this latter place a meeting of the rifle club
was called in honor of Mr. Farrow's
appearance among them. So early in the
season the firing points at the range were
out of order with the exception of that at
the 1100 yards; at this extreme distance
the bull's eye appears one of the tiniest
black specks and barely discernible. It
was a pleasant day and the conditions were

very favorable for fine shooting.   Catching
the correct elevation on the start, Mr. Farrow put in four successive bull's eyes.   The
next shot was a close four; then followed
eight successive bull's eyes, when owing to
a radical change in the conditions, the last
two shots resulted in but four and three.
The total, however, was seventy-one in a
possible seventy-five which is, as far as we
can learn, the highest on record for fifteen
shots at this extreme distance.   From
Springfield to Chicago and Milwaukee,
then Detroit, and from there straight home.

On this trip Mr. Farrow was instrumental
in establishing a number of rifle clubs, both
at long and short range, and the many
gentlemen and sportsmen that he met whose
friendship he acquired, will form a pleasant
reminder for years to come.

Mr. Farrow having been absent so long
during the season of 1880, his off-hand
shooting became somewhat neglected,
especially the German, with heavy rifles and
hair-triggers, he also holding the "King's
medal" and consequently first position, or

place, in this style of shooting; all this induced a desire on the part of some devotees of this sport, pretty well advanced in the art, to arrange a match with the champion, and, if possible, wrest the honor and position from his keeping   It was quietly made up, a subscription match, entrance fee ten dollars each, one hundred shots on the German target of three-fourth inch rings.   There were eight competitors and each one felt at least the ability to carry off *first* or *second*.

The match was contested at Union Hill on the twenty-second of February, 1881. The entrance money was divided into forty, thirty, twenty and ten per cent.   Some very remarkable shooting was the result of this match.   The bull's eye or black at which the aim is taken, measures twelve inches in diameter.   The ring on the outer edge of this bull's eye counts eighteen, and so inward to the very centre, which is one and one-half inches in diameter, counting twenty-five, the highest possible to be attained in one shot.

The match was tallied in scores of ten shots. Mr. Farrow's totals are as follows: 210, 220, 225, 220, 220, 223, 211, 222, 217, 228. The grand total is 2,196, leading the next competitor by 62 rings.

Mr. Farrow's lowest shots in this competition were three seventeens, thus missing the twelve-inch black or bull's eye but three times in the 100 shots.

Learning in the following July of the bi-annual meeting of the Northwestern "Schutzenbund" in St. Paul, Minnesota, and receiving some letters of invitation from members of the society, Mr. Farrow determined, if possible, to organize a team and visit the Western city; it was through his efforts that the team was made up, although going out merely as a member thereof.

The shooting was under the usual conditions of a German "Fest," heavy rifles, hair triggers, peep and globe sights; hand rests also were allowed with which to support the rifles. There were special prizes offered for the marksman that should com-

plete on the "Point Target" the first one
hundred points, also the second hundred
and third hundred.

The honors in this style of shooting had
generally been carried off by a certain
Western marksman, and it was decided
among the members of our team that some
of us should try and win these premiums.
It is usual for every marksman to be present
on the first day of these meetings and make
an attempt to win the medal for the first
one hundred points.   Target accommoda-
tions were limited, which frequently occasioned much unavoidable crowding and
jostling in the endeavors of the marksmen
to reach the firing points.   It was evident
that the shooter who could accomplish the
greatest number of shots at the target in a
certain time would be quite sure to win the
first medal, and it was apparent that any
rifleman who could induce his friends to
give way for him, would have greatly the
advantage over others that had to take their
regular turn.   It happened on this first day
that the corner of the shooting house occu-

pied by the Eastern marksmen was very much crowded; discovering this disadvantage after a few shots, Mr. Farrow moved his traps to the far end of the building where a less number of marksmen were competing; here was found a number of the most prominent Western shooters busy at work and quite far ahead in their scores, occasioned by their more rapid shooting Their lead was too great to be overcome for the first one hundred points, but the second one hundred and also the third one hundred were first attained by Mr. Farrow, who gradually gained on these gentlemen until, when his third one hundred was announced, it was some half an hour or more afterwards before the next shooter completed the same number of points.

The team match was a spirited affair in which the team from the East won first prize; and the members of the team in the individual matches also won many fine prizes, Mr. Farrow taking first on the Creedmoor target, with a fine forty-seven in a possible fifty, the score ending up with six bull's eyes.   This ended the shooting at St. Paul, the remainder of the team returning to the East well satisfied with their excursion to the Western city. Intending to take a trip through the extreme Northwest to test and introduce a new "magazine" rifle, Mr. Farrow started for Montana.   After stopping at several minor points on the route the end of the railroad was reached at a place called Glendive, on the Yellowstone river.

Chapter XII.

Here Mr. Farrow will tell us of his movements.

I arrived at Glendive quite late in the afternoon. I had detected along the railway a gradual loss of the comforts of civilization, especially in the hotels and at the dining houses at the stations where we stopped to refresh the wants of the inner man, but I was hardly prepared for the sudden change or "drop" that I met with at Glendive. From the point where the cars stopped, one could see in the distance a few scattering huts and houses with canvas roofs, and sprinkled here and there some tents. Horses and men were standing around and so mingled or mixed up together that the idea struck my mind each one was apparently in readiness for rapid flight, if necessary, to elude the descent of some band of savages. We were in fact on the verge of civilization. I was recalled to my senses by the familiar tones: "Have a hack? have a hack?" Quickly giving my check to the driver, I mounted the buckboard and we started for the "Grand Pacific Hotel," which the driver so loudly proclaimed to be first class in every respect. We drew up in front of a low log house with a canvas roof, through the open door of which I could see a bar with the shining bottles and glasses behind it. It occurred to me that the driver had stopped to take a drink; with a gentle shake of the head and an admonitory wink, I intimated to him I did not care to "take anything," but he soon dispelled my delusion on the subject as he shouted out, "Here you are, sir, Grand Pacific Hotel." It was with feelings of great disgust that I stepped down from the buckboard and advanced to the door-step of this one story "Grand Pacific." I was about to enter the door when the driver of the buckboard shouted, "Fifty cents, if you please." "Oh!" said I, "that is all right, put it in the bill." He replied that he had no connection with the house, he wanted the money down. Satisfying him, I entered the building. Imagine if you can a log house, some twenty or thirty feet long, with a bar nearly one-half the length in the back centre, with doors on the right leading to the dining-room and kitchen, and on the left to the sleeping rooms, all under a cloth roof, with rough rafters and boards overhead, no laths or plastering or paper of any kind to stop the rude drafts of the cool night wind.

"Will you have some supper?" was asked me by a gentleman whom I supposed to be the proprietor. Assenting to this invitation, I followed him to the dining-room; here the same primitive character pertained to every furnishing of this department. Tables of rough boards nailed together, without cloth or napkins, iron knives and forks, deeply pitted with rust, stationary board seats running along the sides of each table, was sufficient to thoroughly impress a stranger from the East, or, as they term a man from that locality, a "tender-foot," with the idea that he was travelling in a dream and the illusion might soon pass away, or at least he hoped that it would. Once more I was roused from dreamland by the voice of a female of some two hundred pounds weight or more, whose foreign accent, as she cried, "Hash or smash, hot or cowld?" betrayed at once her nationality. Scarcely knowing what I replied, I attempted to realize as much as possible the actual state of society into which I had fallen. The "hash or smash, the hot or cowld," were placed before me, but what it was I cannot state to this day, although I was forced to eat something to maintain existence. On leaving the dining-room, the person whose kindly invitation I had accepted, remarked to me, "Fifty cents, if you please." This I handed him without a murmur and inquired if I could have a room to myself.

"You are mighty lucky if you get a bed all to yourself to-night. We are plum full."

"Well! Do you arrange for the lodgings?"

"No." "You will have to see 'Sleepy Bill' about that; he runs the beds."

And this is the arrangement of the "Grand Pacific," I mentally ejaculated as I moved to the door. Soon I heard the puffing of a steamer on the river. Not wishing to pass more time in Glendive than was necessary I went down to the landing and engaged passage for Miles City. I was fortunate enough to find an unoccupied berth. The next morning we started up the river. The passage to Miles City is usually accomplished in two or three days, but the water being so very low it was nearly a week before we arrived at the end of the journey.

The Merchants Hotel at this place was indeed a "haven of rest." The few days passed in this city were agreeably spent in the company of such gentlemen as my business relations brought me in contact with, some of whom were ardent sportsmen and took great interest in rifle shooting at targets as well as game.

I had a great desire to see what sort of

practical shooting at a 200 yards' target, scouts and hunters by profession, could make with their favorite weapons; and an invitation was given out to all that desired, to attend a competition at 200 yards on the following afternoon, to be held by a celebrated rifle shot from the East, on the vacant lot near the brewery. Quite a large crowd of teamsters, hunters, scouts and ranchmen, with a sprinkling of officers from Fort Keough, were on hand to witness and take part in the shooting. The target was of the regular Creedmoor pattern for 200 yards, four feet wide and six feet high, with eight inch bull's eye. After a few preparatory shots the practice was begun, and in many cases did the hunters and scouts astonish the celebrated shot and themselves, at the ease and frequency with which they could *miss*, not only the bull's eye, but the entire target.

The sheriff of the county was the only one to make an average of centres in ten shots, off-hand. I here learned for the first time that the hunter and scout of books and novels was a far different creature from the hunter and scout of the plains.

This latter person, in a majority of the cases, was a most ordinary looking personage, and invariably if a chance for a shot presented itself and there was no convenient stump or rock, tree or bush to rest his rifle against, a kneeling position was assumed, or one flat upon the ground with both elbows resting; there was none of that high, standing up position, with elbow aimed at the rising sun, left arm extended along the barrel with the "freezing" of the rifle at the object aimed at. Not at all. In its place was the low, crawling. painstaking "Stalker," who hesitated not, to get every advantage over the object of pursuit. Even to fire at a prairie dog, forty yards distant, did I see these noble hunters and scouts down on their knees to take a rest, and *miss* the little fellow at that.

Having business at Fort Buford it was with feelings of regret I left Miles City behind, I had experienced the kindest treatment from the sportsmen there, and the gentlemen at the Fort, whose quarters I had visited and whose hospitalities I had enjoyed.

Fort Buford is a trading station, situated at the junction of the Yellowstone and Missouri rivers. I was detained some days waiting for a steamboat that would stop here on its way to Fort Benton, the head of navigation on the Missouri river, which point I was desirous of making as early in the season as possible, to avoid the snow storms that almost invariably occur in the stage trip over the mountains. The steamer General Terry soon put in an appearance, and I was comfortably quartered by the clerk, who knew me very well by reputation and expressed great pleasure in being able to make my acquaintance. "We will have some rare fun going up the river. We shall meet with plenty of buffalo and deer," he remarked. "Nothing could suit me better," and we both set out for the supper table.

At this season of the year the water in the Missouri is at a very low ebb, and steamboats in the carrying trade up that stream, travel very carefully and only during the day, frequently getting stuck on sand bars for hours, and having to push or "pole" themselves as they call it, over or away from the obstruction, by the means of spars attached to the forward part of the boat, worked by a steam capstan or "Nigger" as it is technically called on board.

At the end of the first week I began to feel a little anxious to catch a glimpse of the buffalo or deer promised me by the clerk, and on intimating to him the fact, he expressed great surprise at our not having seen any. It was seldom on a trip up the river they did not see many buffalo, either crossing the river at some narrow place or wallowing in the mud at the river banks. The boat being heavily laden our passage up the shallow water was so slow we were overtaken by one or two steamboats coming up behind.

An amusing incident happened at this point which might be interesting to some of my readers, which I will try to relate exactly as it occurred.

The General Terry was slowly crawling over a sand bar as the steamer Penina came puffing along, loaded with a detachment of troops and some government material, destined for a point farther up the river. Sticking fast to the bar, her captain signalled our craft, lowered a boat and came on board. Accompanying him was a tall, dark personage with a rifle in one hand and a bag of tools in the other. He ascended to the saloon deck, familiarly addressed the clerk, who answered with the salutation :

"How are you, Cherokee Jim?"

"Well, I'm movin' "

"So I see," answered the clerk. "Bag and baggage too, hey?"

"Well," he replied, "I was in a hurry to git up the river and thought I'd change boats."

Our lamented President's story of "swapping horses while crossing the stream" occurred to my mind at the moment of hearing this conversation, but I said nothing.

We soon steamed on our way up the river, leaving the Penina sticking fast on the bar. It was a beautiful afternoon, scarcely a cloud in sight, and the passengers were out on deck enjoying the scenery which was quite rugged at this point of the river. Cherokee Jim, I learned afterwards, was a half-breed, well known on the Missouri by all the steamboat men, and was considered a fair scout and an excellent shot; but of a surly disposition when in his cups and "half seas over." He had brought his magazine rifle on deck and seemed stimulated with a desire to exhibit to the passengers his skill in shooting. After firing a shot or two he was interrupted by the clerk, who went up to him and remarked:

"You think you can shoot some, don't you, Jim?"

"Well, I reckon I ain't afraid to tackle anythin' on the Missouri."

"Oh pooh!" said the clerk, "We have got a man on board who shoots birds flying, with a rifle ball."

"That's a chance shot," said Cherokee Jim. "No man can hit birds with a bullet right along."

"Nonsense," retorted the clerk. "I tell you we have;" and turning to me, he said, "Say! Mr. Farrow, where is your rifle?" "There is no use showing my rifle by the side of this one the gentleman has got." was my answer as I stepped forward.

"What is your gun?" I asked of the half-breed. "A magazine?"

"Yes, and a better gun *never spit lead.*"

"Let me see it?"

He handed me the piece with the remark that it was loaded. I examined the gun carefully, tried the pull of the trigger.

"It goes easy," he said. I remarked that "it was all right."

We were standing by the side of the boat well forward on the saloon deck; two boxes of empty beer bottles were in the corner formed by the railing. I intimated to one of the passengers that if he would throw in the air an empty beer bottle I would try to break it. With an inquiring look at the clerk, who nodded his head in answer, the gentleman pulled out the bottle, and with a long sweep of the arm gave it a toss in the air; the bottle rose some five or six feet above the level of our heads, and as it paused for an instant in turning for its fall, I caught a quick aim through the sights and fired. The bottle flew into a thousand pieces.

"A chance shot! a chance shot!" cried Cherokee Jim, who had expected I would shoot at the bottle as it floated in the water.

"There's another ketridge in that gun; give him another one," he remarked, very quickly. "I will throw it up," said the clerk, whereupon he took up a bottle and with a quick jerk threw it almost straight into the air. Having practiced at breaking glass balls with a rifle at home, I was "well on" to such shots as the clerk gave me in this instance, and this bottle shared the fate of the preceding one.

"Have you another cartridge?" I asked of the Cherokee.

"Yes, yes," he remarked, somewhat excitedly, and he handed me two. I loaded the rifle, one shot in the magazine and the other in the chamber.

"Let me throw up one?" said Cherokee, and he stepped to the box where the bottles were and drew out *two*, one in each hand. I "dropped," as they say out West, on his idea, and was prepared.

"Here you go!" he cried: "One, two, three," and up went one bottle immediately followed by the other. The first one went up at an angle of about forty-five degrees; this I was prepared for, and catching good aim it was broken almost instantly. The other bottle had apparently slipped somewhat from his grasp and did not ascend as high in the air as was anticipated, but quickly began to fall; by a rapid movement of the lever, I threw out the empty shell and inserted the loaded cartridge with the return motion, and at the same time following the dropping glass-ware, I instinctively pulled the trigger, shattering the empty beer receptacle into fragments only a foot above the water. A hearty round of applause from the passengers and crew ensued, at the conclusion of which the Cherokee, who actually looked *pale* at the successful breaking of the bottles, shouted out, "By Gee, pard, give us your hand; let's take a drink, what'll you hev?" And without more ado, as it was impossible to get away from the *enthused* scout, we all repaired to the store-room where each partook of the fluid of that character which had filled the bottles we had just destroyed. The Cherokee was never tired of repeating: "Well, that *was* shooting," whenever any allusion to my skill with the rifle was made the subject of conversation.

Our voyage up the river continued as slow and tedious as before. At the end of fourteen days from the time of my entry on the boat, we had ascended the river as far as was possible to proceed, owing to the low state of the water. The point on the river at which we were forced to land was some one hundred and seventy odd miles from Fort Benton, and one hundred and nineteen miles nearly due North from the river to Fort Assiniboine.

On the morning of the day when the captain decided we could proceed no further, he informed me of the fact and intimated that I should be forced to land with the freight or go back down the river.

Looking ashore to the river bank, I could see no signs of habitation, no houses or tents of any kind, but far up from the river, near where the bluff rises so abruptly, was the resting place of two squatters, who depended upon their hunting, and also their wood cutting ability to supply the passing steamers with fuel, for their livelihood. I remarked to the captain, it seemed rather a dreary situation, to say the least. I had a valise weighing a trifle over one hundred pounds, two heavy rifles and some ammunition. It was a question with me how I was to be transported, with this amount of luggage, to some one of the many stations reached by the mail stage. On mentioning this to the captain, he replied, if I remained at the bank long enough a "bull train," as he called it, "would soon arrive from the fort to load up with freight. I could then return with the train and find the stage at that point."

This was very poor comfort for me; I was anxious, if possible, to catch an *express* train. It was getting late in the season, the evenings had shown a chilliness that was far from agreeable, even when provided with the light coverings on the steamboat, but there was nothing better to be done.

After a rude protection from the rain and cold had been arranged, the goods and supplies for the fort were landed. I saw the steamer disappear behind a point lower down on the stream; it brought to mind ideas that were engendered by reminiscences of places on the river, pointed out to me by the clerk, as made memorable by skirmishes with the Indians, which had been fatal to many of the hardy squatters and trappers of that region.

"Suppose a band of Indians should appear, come down, as it were, from the high bluffs that guard the river bank?"

"No fear of that," said a voice near me. Turning around, the kindly face of one of the before mentioned squatters was pre-

sented to my view. I was quite unaware
of having expressed my thoughts in an
audible tone till startled by the scout. I
began a conversation with the squatter and
learned that this cattle train was expected
over from the fort in about a week, also
that he and his "pard" were going out on
a hunt for some buffalo meat. The steamboat had gone down the river to get part
of the freight that had been landed some
fifty miles below, at a place where great
difficulty was experienced in getting over a
bar. An invitation to "go along and get a
shot at big game"—not having seen either
deer or buffalo on the entire journey up the
river—was a pleasing surprise, which I
accepted at once, for a chance to pass the
time of waiting in so agreeable a manner
was not to be neglected.

In the morning we started the "outfit," a
large covered wagon drawn by four horses,
and indeed it required their full strength to
pull the nearly empty vehicle up the steep
bluff. After arriving at the summit, the
table land appeared stretching out broad

and level as far as the eye could see, with
Bear Paw mountains, as I was informed,
rising from the horizon. The eastern end
of this range of mountains was our point of
destination, and it was late in the afternoon
before we arrived near enough to discover
with the glass any indications of the
buffalo.

The plains at that time were very dry,
no rain having fallen for a long period.
The hunters were striving to reach a point
at the base of the mountains, near a small
stream of water; we were sure to find some
buffalo near, as they can hardly exist without this refreshing beverage. After a long
search with the field glasses, one of the
hunters remarked, " Five buffalo I see at
the head of that ravine. *There* is some
water; we will camp there tonight."

I said to the hunter: " Cannot we get a
shot at those fellows this evening?"

" Rather hard work," he replied. " The
ground is very open."

" Suppose you try the bed of the stream
for the wagon, you and I start ahead; that

point will cover our approach up to two hundred yards."

"It seems a good idea," he replied, and we immediately got down and started off on foot; as we came in sight of the animals, he remarked, "All old bulls, not good for meat, too old, no use to go any further," but I was too anxious to get a shot to heed this admonition, and urged him to go on.

"So you want to kill a buffalo?"

"That's what I do," I answered in the Plains vernacular that I was unconsciously assuming; a natural consequence of living in the Northwest.

"Well! I'll give you a chance." And here I will say I *was* anxious to get a shot at a buffalo, or even a deer; it had been mentioned quite a number of times on the steamboat: "These *tenderfeet* target shooters that come out in this country and try to shoot game, generally find a big difference," and they had attacks of "buck fever" or nervous prostration of some kind, which seriously interfered with any hunting on their part," etc., etc. I anxious was

to study my own condition when brought
face to face with, and a certainty of, a shot
at big game.

With a careful glance at the magazine
rifle in my hand, to see the hammer was
on the safety notch, I prepared to follow
the hunter, who had started off in a crouch-
ing position; it was still necessary to keep
from sight of the buffalo. It took some
time to stalk these animals and arrive near
enough to make a sure shot. We were
now running in the creek bed, then crawling on hands and knees through the
" brush," then as the buffalo dropped their
heads to feed, a quick run of a few yards
to another friendly shelter; in this way we
were able to approach within seventy or
eighty yards of the nearest animal; he was
standing with broad side presented, his
head lowered to the ground, feeding on
the short grass, wholly unaware of the
approach of any enemy.

"Now," said the scout, "we must shoot
from here; aim low down behind the fore-
shoulder." I was raising my rifle to shoot

"off-hand," with the left arm extended in true hunters' style, but he stopped me with "Take a rest, take a rest over your knee." I waited a moment to see if I was actually nervous, or if any signs of "buck fever" were present, but any nervousness, more than what would be naturally occasioned by the violent exercise that we had just taken in arriving at this point, was not discernible.

"What distance do you think it is?"

"Near a hundred yards," he said.

Arranging my sight for the distance designated, I raised the weapon to my shoulder, as if shooting at the target at two hundred yards, set the pin head low down on the shoulder and pulled the trigger. With a loud snort and jump, each buffalo started to run. The one I had shot at began to limp; it was not over fifty yards before he stopped and began to swing himself in a circle and then pitched over on one side. "Sit down, sit down, we may get a stand on them." "What is that?" I asked. He explained to me that the buffalo hunters

often conceal themselves near the centre of
the herd, and after the fright occasioned
by the first shot, not knowing which way
to flee from the danger, they became terri-
fied to such a degree as to run hither and
thither and round about, until the hunts-
man had killed sometimes half the entire
herd. After peeping over the bushes he
said, "It's no use to wait for these old bulls,
they are taking up on to the bluffs above the
creek; will you take another shot at
them?" With a remark about the distance
I raised my sight for a longer range. The
animals had now paused upon the top of
the bank and were looking down at the
creek bottom for their fallen comrade.
"Why! they wait for him," I said. "Yes,"
he answered, "they hesitate, and if it were
younger cattle would soon return, but these
old bulls are too well educated; now is
your time to shoot if you will try again."
There were two animals standing near
each other. I aimed for the centre of their
black shaggy coats, and fired; the dust
flew from the alkaline soil in a direct line

with the buffalo, but some twenty yards short, as the bullet whistled over their heads in its rebound. It was an amusing sight to watch the heavy creatures, with their tails in the air, snorting and bellowing, rush off in rapid flight.

"A good liner, but too low." We advanced to the side of our fallen game. "He is not dead yet; the bullet struck him too high up," said the hunter. The animal lay upon its side, kicking and panting, the blood flowing from his nostrils, and exhausting himself with vain endeavors to get upon its feet. "It is indeed an old bull," the hunter remarked, after an examination of his horns. "Fifteen years old, if a day." Going behind the animal I administered the *coup de grace* in the shape of a bullet in the back of his neck; his struggles ceased instantaneously; the lead had penetrated to the very seat of life.

Taking the buffalo's scalp and leaving the entire carcass except the tongue, we started back for the wagon, which by this time was in sight. We camped in the

creek bed, were up long before daybreak
and on our way. It was necessary we
should reach the stream of water early in
the morning; we should find more buffalo
near at that time than in any other part of
the day.

When light enough to use the glass, the
hunter, after a careful search, remarked,
" Plenty of buffalo, can see at least five
hundred." Concealing the wagon behind
a projecting bluff, we took our way to the
vicinity of the springs; we were not disappointed in finding the game, but of the
entire herd not one of the female gender
could be seen. " It will be hard to find
anything but old bulls in this herd," said
the scout. " Did you see those five?" I
inquired, referring to some animals near
the foot of a spur that seemed to jut out
into the creek bottom. " Where?" he said.
I pointed them out to him and he answered,
" We can get at those, come this way."
We made a detour to the right, then
ascended the side of the bluff; it was some
forty or fifty feet to the top. We then

started round to follow this point to the
end, where the buffalo appeared to be feeding. As we approached the edge and
looked over, the animals were standing at
the foot of the declivity, looking around
and snuffing as if their sense of smell gave
them evidence of the proximity of danger. "They have got our wind," said the
scout. I then noticed for the first time
the wind blew from the direction of our
camp. "Are you ready?" he inquired.
I peered over the bank, and as I looked
down the leader of the band was apparently looking in my direction. "Shall I
take him right between the eyes?" "No,
no, don't shoot there, the bullet will glance
off." Noting the angle at which the animal's forehead appeared, I saw at once the
truth of this. "Shoot him close to the
neck, and range the bullet well *down;* that
is the best shot to make." Comprehending
his idea on the instant, I deliberately
placed the front sight low down on the animal's neck and fired. They all started off
with their usual alacrity, and as I reloaded

my rifle the scout fired. A cloud of dust flew up behind one of the buffalo. " Missed him," was all he said. At the rapid flight of the game I fancied a shot gun was in my hand and it would seem that the buffalo were birds; glancing through the sight and leading the now flying animals, as is the rule in making a "crossing-shot" at a bird, I pressed the trigger; a dull *thud* from the bullet as it struck the animal's side was plainly discernible. " You've hit him, you have hit," said the scout, and a second buffalo began to limp in a terribly painful manner; all soon disappeared around the bluff point. "Now," said the hunter, "we'll cut them off on the other side." We started on the double quick for the further edge of the bluff; reaching the spot before me he sat down, deliberately raised his rifle, and fired again at the passing herd; there were but four of them now, one having fallen down, the first shot proving his death wound. To seat myself beside him I placed my hand, not on the ground, as I expected but oh! horror! I had pressed my open palm into the very heart of a cactus plant. The excruciating agony that followed, induced by the ten thousand spines from this prickly pear, was such that I knew not of the flight of the buffalo or of the shots from the hunter's rifle. Any one who has ever met with an experience of this kind will pardon, without hesitation, some few remarks made at the moment as to the origin and character of this particular cactus, but I am under the impression that the atmosphere was " mephitic " and of a " cerulean hue." " Our army swore terribly in Flanders."

We pursued the band no further, the two buffalo already slain proved quite acceptable, and after dressing, as much as our horses could draw to the river.

After three more days of waiting, the " bull train " or " mule train," which it proved to be, was ready to start. This mule train, and it was no exception to the general rule, was made up of some twelve " teams," with four mules to each team, which consisted of two wagons, that is, the head wagon, or leader, to which the mules were attached, had affixed to its rear a trail team of the same size, both being loaded with supplies or merchandize. This entire train was loaded with boxes of bottled beer, although on the river bank were barrels of flour, sacks of oats, bacon, and eatables of different kinds; the necessity of providing "something to drink" for tne fort was of more importance, at this time, than the conveyance of the more solid provisions. It was two days before the train was raised to the table land, only to be reached by the trail leading up the steep bluff. The travelling then was more easy. We expected to make twenty miles the next day.

We accomplish a good start and go into camp early. A circle is formed by the wagons as they are placed for the night with an opening at each end; the mules are unharnessed and allowed to wander at will, while one of the company, called the "night herder," watches them, lest they stray away in the darkness. The morning feed of oats is well remembered by each animal, and long before the break of day their clamorings for the expected meal break in upon the sleep of the most tired driver.

It was in this way we journeyed till within two days' drive of Assiniboine. The provisions had gradually been growing less in quantity and of poorer quality, and it actually got so low and so bad the entire company "struck," and would not harness a mule or make any start or effort towards reaching their destination. After a "council of war" was held, in which the overseer of the train used language more expressive than elegant, he started for Assiniboine on "mule-back" for relief in the shape of flour and other provision to feed the "outfit."

Here we were impressively reminded of the lines from the ancient mariner, "Water, water everywhere, and not a drop to drink." Here was "beer, beer everywhere," but nothing to eat and our "souls yearned," or our stomachs did, for those provisions we had left on the banks of the river.

It was some days after this before the train arrived at the fort. I had a letter of introduction to the commandant, Major Morris, who, with his estimable wife, received me with cordial and generous hospitality; and I invariably found and received the most cordial treatment from the different commanders and officers at the various stations and posts that it was my good fortune to visit.

CHAPTER XIII.

I found at the *fort* another surprise in waiting. All my ideas of frontier fortifications had been formed from what I had seen of forts on the sea coast in the East, and I expected to see at least some *signs* of a fortification or defensive positions built up of logs or earth works. My surprise may well be imagined to find, instead, one of the most beautifully arranged government stations, not only for the concentration of troops, but arranged for their comfort and convenience in every detail. I saw a wide open square somewhat longer than wide in its proportions ; at the one end was a handsome brick building constituting the hospital, at the opposite end a trader's store ; on the eastern side were the officers' dwellings, beginning on the right with the commandants and ending with the chapel and school-room ; whilst on the other side were the soldiers' quarters—a row of long houses of two-story construction, with a piazza running the full length of each. In the rear of these last mentioned buildings were the stables for the horses and the quarters for the scouts, with which each Western force is more or less provided, and greatly depended on by the military in their skirmishes and warfare with the Indians.

All of these houses and buildings were of brick, built in modern style, and with all the conveniences that were possible at that distance from refined civilization.

The Fort, as it is called, was situated near the arm of a creek, or river, but upon the level table land without protection in the way of raised embankments or embrasures of any kind such as I expected to find.

The view across the level plain is unobstructed, and the distant mountains, some of them snow capped, apparently rise from the horizon fifty to sixty miles away.

Fort Assiniboine is some sixty-five miles from Fort Benton, and is the end of the stage line; the stage goes no further, and, in fact, there is no other inhabited place for hundreds of miles for it to go to. The mails for the fort, which come twice a week, are carried by this line.

Leaving Assiniboine at five in the morning, if parties are taken through on time, and not delayed by some sudden snow storm or squall of wind and rain which frequent the plains at this season of the year, they arrive at Benton late in the afternoon. This is a town of some importance, having a daily paper, telegraph office and other conveniences that had been left far behind. It is also the highest point on the Missouri to which steamboats ascend, which they can only do in the early season when the water is high. There I found some congenial spirits that were interested in shooting, both with the rifle and shot gun. Deer, antelope and buffalo were somewhat scarce at that season of the year, but I was assured by one of the prominent sportsmen of some of the finest duck shooting that could be had in

the United States.   Fifteen miles from Fort
Benton were some lakes which are the
stopping places of thousands of ducks and
geese in their annual migrations.   If I
would go along my informant promised to
lend me a shot gun and take me with a
couple of his friends to spend a day among
the ducks.   I was too willing to accept the
genial invitation.   It was soon after dinner
that he came to the hotel for me; I was
prepared to take my rifle and a supply of
cartridges along, but he informed me it
would be only "baggage in the way" as
I would have no occasion whatever to use
them.   "We have plenty of guns and
ammunition," he said, "so take your
blankets, shooting coat and jump in;" this
advice I followed.   We were soon spin-
ning along the table land to which we had
ascended; the town being situated on the
north side of the river bottom, which at
this place is a mile and a half wide.   We
stopped at a ranch on the way and "lubricated the inner man," as one gentleman
expressed it, and I found it was a part of

the regular programme with these Western people, especially those engaged in out-of-door pursuits, to " lubricate this inner man " somewhat extensively. Not being able to support much of this " lubrication," I partook somewhat sparingly. We then resumed our journey to the lakes; it was some time after sunset before we arrived at our camping place, so we got no ducks that day. In the morning I found we needed no decoys or boats; the ducks were there in countless numbers and constantly flying across a narrow isthmus of land that separated the two lakes. We were concealed in blinds built of bushes and grass and took our choice of shots as the birds flew over us. After exhausting my ammunition and getting well tired of the constant pounding of the light ten-gauge gun, I proposed to " take a rest." The other gentlemen were still deeply engaged in the sport and had no desire to give it up, but upon a proposition to take some luncheon, which had been brought along, all started for the wagon, which was some distance from the lakes, sheltered by a point or bluff. We enjoyed our repast with keen appetites, brought on by the exercise and bracing air; we had nearly finished when I inquired, "Are not buffalo and deer sometimes found in this vicinity?" "Oh! occasionally they are seen." "Well," said I, "Are those cattle over there near the point of that bluff?" pointing to one a short distance away. "No, there is no cattle ranch around here; it must be buffalo." The attention of our party being directed to the point, all declared three were plainly in sight. Addressing one of the party, I said, "Let you and I see if we can catch a buffalo." With a hearty laugh he answered that the buffalo would catch us, and added, "There are no buffalo guns in the outfit." "O! yes," said another, "I have a 'Springfield' in the wagon and some cartridges." Hinting that I would like to go and take a shot at them, he assured me I was quite welcome and said he would come along with me and thus save his shot cartridges for the afternoon flight of ducks   We were soon on our way, I with the Springfield, and he with his shot gun and heavy revolver. It was some two miles to where we had seen the buffalo, which were feeding near the entrance of a ravine into which they were slowly disappearing. We took a direct line across the table land to intercept them at the further end of the opening. Nearing the locality we found numerous "wash-outs," or gullies, which were cut deep into the ground by the melting of snow and the heavy rains. The sides of these wash-outs were very steep and in some places we could not easily climb them, but succeeded by pressing the edges of the heavy soles of our boots into the hard alkaline soil. After crossing a number of these "gullies," we arrived at the end of the ravine and peered over. Two of the buffalo only were in sight. My companion, who had had some experience, said to me : "This is a fine point, the buffalo will come this way ; you remain here and I will make a detour and start them from the opposite side."

The plan succeeded most admirably. I waited at the point indicated and when my friend showed himself on the opposite side at the entrance of the ravine, the nearest buffalo started directly for my hiding place. The wind, unfortunately for me, was in a direction that gave the scent to the animal as he was ascending the bank of the ravine. When nearly half way to the top, he stopped, snuffing and stamping, and glaring fiercely in my direction with a distance of scarcely fifty yards between us; his tail was elevated and switching angrily from side to side. Resting my elbow on my knee I, with cool deliberation, pointed the rifle exactly between his eyes and fired.

At the result of the shot I was somewhat astonished. The buffalo, with a louder snort, turned completely around, and looked down the declivity, which he had partly ascended, with all the fierceness and earnestness that he had before exhibited when glaring in my direction. It was a few seconds before I could explain this change of front on the buffalo's part, but as

I looked at him carefully I missed that grand and majestic *switch*, *switch* of the tail that was apparent before the shot. I then perceived, as the buffalo began to turn round and round with extreme vexation, a jangled and tangled or mortified attempt to circulate, as it were, his caudal appendage, which now hung only by the skin, the bullet having passed above the back of the animal and severed the vertebral bone some two or three inches from the body, and the animal being hurt so severely in his rear-most part was as much astonished with pain and vexation as I was at the effects of the bullet, which had gone so high above the aim, from a mistake in the sights, which were set for two hundred yards and not for fifty as I had been informed.

Removing the empty shell from the rifle, I felt in my pockets for another cartridge, but, alas! I find cause for agitation, my friend had the cartridges in his possession; when he handed me the rifle, remarking that it was loaded, he retained the supply of cartridges in his own pocket. I was standing in plain sight of the buffalo, having risen from my position after firing, and being at last perceived by the animal, he made a "bolt" in my direction; as there was nothing else to do I also made a "bolt." Any direction to me was safety if I could only outrun the quadruped. Throwing down the Springfield, as it would only impede my progress, I, in Western phrase, "lighted out for all I was worth." Not more than a hundred yards brought me to the edge of one of the wash-outs, and glancing behind I saw the buffalo had full steam on and was doing his utmost to overtake me. The side of the wash-out at this point was very steep. Without hesitation though I plunged down, and reaching the other bank tried to ascend, but the angle of the incline was so sharp, and being somewhat out of breath from my exertions, I could only make a partial ascent of the acclivity and take advantage of a seam or slight projection, dig hands and feet into the earth, and thus sustain myself at this point, about half way to the top. The distance from side to side of this wash-out was not more than forty or fifty feet. The buffalo coming to the place at which I had disappeared and seeing me on the opposite side, without hesitation jumped and scrambled to the bottom, and with an angry rush and roar tried to climb to where I was. I was up some fifteen or twenty feet from the bottom of the wash-out and the buffalo, as he tore the dirt with his horns and tried to reach me, was scarcely more than three or four feet below my resting place.*

How long it would have been before he had undermined my position, owing to the amount of earth he was tearing up, and brought me down to his level I cannot say, but my feelings were somewhat relieved by a loud shout from my friend who had hastened to the rescue, he having seen the charge of the buffalo and my rapid flight; he also noticed my abandonment of the

---

*It may be notorious that buffalos cannot climb trees, but I can say without any hesitation that I entertain a very respectful idea of their ability to get up a steep bank, or climb the sides of a "wash-out."

Springfield and, knowing all tne ammunition was in his own possession, he started to regain the rifle and come to my assistance.

Giving an answering "hallo" to apprize him of my situation, he soon came in sight further down the side of the wash-out. Recognizing the fact at once that it was impossible for the buffalo to come up on either side, he boldly advanced to the bank above and began a fusilade on the animal. The buffalo at the first shot turned from me and tried to ascend the opposite bank, but the bullets from the Springfield were too much for him and he soon turned over and rolled to the bottom of the gully, a helpless mass.

It might be proper to say here, as a final and fitting end to this remarkable chase, that on my way home from the lakes I was triumphantly awarded "*the brush*."

From Fort Benton to Helena the distance is about one hundred and eighty miles. The stage, which is the only public conveyance, travels night and day with the mail. I was informed that the passage over the mountains was made in the night, and at that season of the year the cold was intense, owing to the high altitude reached as we followed the trail. We had scarcely got clear from Benton before fine particles of snow began to fall, and long before night we were pushing our way through a driving storm. The temperature had fallen some twenty degrees during the last few hours; however, we pressed on, and by nightfall the snow had covered the level plain to the depth of some six or eight inches.

It was long after dark when we began the first ascent of the mountain; the range at this place, I learned from the driver, was the dividing point of the water sheds; we were now on the Atlantic side and as soon as we crossed the summit we should be on the Pacific slope. The altitude at which we crossed the divide was nearly seven thousand feet, and if on time we would arrive at the top about twelve o'clock.

It proved in this case to be much later.

The snow had driven into the road and blocked the way to such an extent that our progress was very much impeded and became slower and slower, and for most of the distance to the top it was nearly to the hubs of the wheels, and two hours were required to make the pull of the last half mile.

Here the thermometer had gone below zero, and the scanty covering for protection from the cold, with which the passengers were provided, occasioned very much suffering, and I will say that of all the nights of discomfort that it was ever my experience to endure this was the most fearful.

We were obliged to remain at the next station, where we changed horses, two days for the snow to melt sufficiently that we could proceed on our journey.

As it was impossible to hold any shooting competition or matches in such weather as this, after a sojourn at Helena sufficiently long to recover from the severe cold contracted in that terrible night's ride over "the Rockies," I took stage for Deer Lodge and Butte City. Fifteen miles from the latter I reached the railroad, and it was with feelings of much joy that I found myself safely on board and hurrying over the rails. Here my sufferings from stage riding came to an end. I proceeded to Salt Lake City and after a happy stay of some days, took my departure for the East.

NOTE.—The following interesting adventure was misplaced in the manuscript. We insert it here, believing it should not be omitted from the book. —[Ed.

I arrived at Bismark too late in the afternoon to make much progress in looking up the sportsmen of the town.

In the morning the clerk of the hotel informed me that one of the editors of the paper was a sportsman and belonged to the club. It was quite a live institution and the members did considerable shooting at glass balls, but indulged very little in rifle practice. I called on this gentleman with my credentials and was apparently well received, but in the afternoon's issue of the paper any notice of my arrival was not to be found. I had meanwhile made the acquaintance of certain other members of the club that were doing business in the place and, although they confessed themselves "no rifle shots," gave me to understand that with the shot gun at glass balls or ducks they felt themselves quite at home in any company. Regretting the fact that I had no shot gun with me, I also intimated I would be delighted at a skirmish with the ducks. One of the gentlemen offered to loan me a gun, and proposed to go in the afternoon down the river bank some two or three miles to the slough where we would find plenty of ducks to be had for the shooting.

This slough, referred to by the sportsman, was a sort of marshy pond, some mile and a half long by three quarters wide, and deep enough through the central part to float a ducking skiff or small boat. I had had one experience in slough shooting for ducks and I inquired if they had any decoys or required a boat. "Oh! no," one answered, "if *you* shoot any ducks we can wade in and get them, the water is not very deep." After thinking the matter over, I provided myself with six long sticks about the size and length of an ordinary ramrod, and sharpened or pointed each end; also two square pieces of board to be extemporized into a seat. As I placed these in the rear end of the wagon, I noticed a slight nudge of the elbow on the part of one sportsman to another, and an indicatory nod in my direction. This elicited an inquiry from the party if I was going to "string my birds on a stick." With the remark that it would not be a bad idea, perhaps, I also intimated that if the ducks presented themselves I could soon place enough of them "*hors du combat*" to fill up the sticks.

There were five in the party, with the driver, who was to take care of the wagon and horses; the rest of us were sportsmen, fully armed and equipped. In a short time we drove up to the side of the slough and the leader of the party remarked, "Mart,

you and I will go down to the left and let
the other gentlemen go around the upper
end; we can meet at the foot and Ned will
have the wagon there for us." "How long
shall we shoot?" "Oh! it will be near
dark before you get through" I shoul-
dered my gun, and with sticks and seat in
hand started for the point indicated. There
was scarcely a ripple upon the water and
as there were no ducks in sight I must say
I was fearful of having made a mistake;
however, I determined to make the best of
it, and when I arrived at the upper end,
where the rushes and grass were growing
in the water and extending some hundred
yards or more, I saw some teal and waded
in; finding the water reached but little
above mid-leg, I continued wading until
some distance from the shore; here I succeeded in killing two of the teal, which I
set up with my pointed sticks in the water
to serve as decoys. A tuft of tall grass
near by making a convenient hiding place
and the water not being very cold, I knew
my position would not be uncomfortable,

provided I was enlivened by an occasional shot. Other parties were after ducks in a boat at the further end of the slough; a distant *bang*, *bang*, assured me of their stirring up the fowl, and I noticed coming from that direction two mallards; as they swung around in my vicinity I captured one of them, although with the second barrel, and placed him as a decoy with the teal. With the start thus begun I soon had some fine shooting and all my sticks set out, each with a dead bird held in place for a decoy. The friends that had accompanied me were having rare sport, to judge from the continued firing, and I began to think my bag would hardly be as heavy as theirs, they being familiar with the ground and could take every advantage.

When darkness approached I gathered up my birds and found that standing in the water so long, had benumbed my extremities to such a degree, I had great difficulty in carrying my game and gun to the land. While waiting for the wagon to drive up, I counted the results of my efforts,—sixteen,

mallard and teal. The other parties were
apprised of my position and knew that I
had remained at this end of the slough. It
was somewhat after dark before they
arrived at the place, and as they drove up
and halted, one of them inquired: "Well,
what luck, Mr. Farrow?" I was anxious
to know the extent of their bag before
replying, so I answered his question in true
Yankee style by asking another, "How
many birds have you got?" "By Gad!"
he says, with some exultation, "we have
got two." "What," said I, "two for the
whole party?" "Yes," he answered, "we
have got two, and if you have got more
than that you have done mighty well."
Upon my assuring him *sixteen* was the
total of my bag, he would not believe it
until he had seen and counted them for
himself. I remarked that some of these
"wandering 'tender-feet' from the East"
were "quite capable with the shot gun or
with the rifle, even if they did take sticks
to string their ducks on." "Now," he continued, "what did you do with the sticks?"

Upon my explaining to him how I had used them by running the pointed end of the stick under the skin, up the neck and through to the top of the head of the dead duck to support it in a life like position as a decoy, he remarked: "That is a down east dodge, and I'll bet money no one but a tender foot would have thought of practicing such a thing around here." "Which one of the New England States did you come from?" was his next inquiry. I told him I was born in the State of Maine. He reached out and shook my hand vigorously with the remark: "How are you Pine Tree State? there's where I belong, too." The drive home was enlivened by the detailed experiences of each one and the bad luck of loosing ducks actually killed, seemed to have followed each individual, with one single exception, for enough ducks were knocked down *dead* during this short drive to have supplied the hotels for a week at least. We soon arrived at the store where a crowd of friends, who knew of our departure, had been impatiently awaiting our return; they began their inquiries as to our success: "How many birds did you get, Mart?" "Oh! I didn't shoot anything." Just then the driver passed out my bunch of ducks. "Oh! you didn't get nothing, whose birds are they?" The driver remarked that "these all belonged to the gentleman from the East." "What," said another, "you let that rifle shot beat you all with your own tools? well! you are a precious lot." "Whose gun did you have?" "How did you do it?" remarked a third, tapping me on the shoulder. The only explanation that I gave was to invite them all in to "Mart's" to take a "lunar," as it was styled in that town, which was more clearly discernible over, and in front of, a long mahogany bar and through the bottom of a tumbler. This explanation was quite satisfactory, and finding the "rifle-shot" such a jolly good fellow, they voted it was no disgrace to be defeated at the hands of such an artist.

The next edition of the paper, however, contained a notice of the arrival of a distinguished rifle shot who was an "ardent sportsman, W. M. Farrow, from the East," with a card ending to the effect that "the boys had better sharpen up their wits as well as their flints."

Chapter XIV.

On arriving at New York, I was informed by letters from Newport that my brother's health had failed him to such an extent he must give up business for the coming season, at least. This necessitated my returning, to once more take charge of the affairs I had left in his care some five years before

During the season, which proved to be a busy one, I found but little time to practice any long-range shooting, two hundred yards being the extent of our range at the club grounds; at this distance I was enabled to keep my practice well in hand; the meetings of our club were held at the range on Wednesday of each week. My return to the city was the occasion of renewed interest being manifested by members and friends of the association, and I felt greatly encouraged in my endeavors to perfect an off-hand team of sufficient skill

that in the coming Fall meeting of the
National Rifle Association at Creedmoor,
we could attend and compete for a respectable position with the crack off-hand clubs
that frequent this famous rifle range.

The visit of a British rifle team had been
assured to the National Rifle Association.
This organization was preparing to raise
a team of marksmen to compete in an
international match against the visitors,
and had issued printed circulars, with conditions attached, requiring certain competitions to be engaged in, to enable any
marksman to become eligible for a place
on the team.   As these conditions required
shooting at the extreme distances of eight
hundred, nine hundred, and one thousand
yards, and there being no accessible range
in this state, I could not conform to these
conditions and become really eligible for a
place on the team.

Having given up any idea of attempting
to gain a position on the team, I was
greatly surprised on a certain day in
August to receive a personal visit from the

Secretary of the Association. He remarked, during a lengthy conversation, that it was his desire and also that of many others of the National Rifle Association, that I should enter the final competitions for the team; my known reputation and skill in public matches, he assured me, were sufficient for waiving the competitions called for in the circular; it would be done, not only in my case, but in the case of some others, also that he would take a trip to Providence to see the Governor and Adjutant General of Rhode Island, and induce them, if possible, to offer a trophy to anyone in the National Guard of the state that should win a position on the team. My strong desire to see the American arms victorious in the coming contest, backed by the personal solicitations of the irresistible Secretary, induced me to give a promise to come to Creedmoor and enter the final competition.

I immediately began practicing with a military rifle at two hundred yards, and made some very good records, forty-five,

forty-six and forty-seven on two or three
different occasions. Not being able to
practice over the longer ranges, that I
might adjust the sights and procure the
proper elevations and windage, I felt some
uneasiness, but promising myself to go to
Creedmoor a week, at least, before the
regular competitions began, to perfect the
ammunition and the arrangement of the
sights for the longer distance, I contented
myself.

But press of business and other circumstances prevented me from going on at the
time I intended, and I was forced to satisfy
myself with but one practice at Creedmoor,
which was accomplished on Monday afternoon from four o'clock to six.

It will be seen that I had time on that
day to shoot but a few shots at the lower
ranges, and in no way could I satisfy
myself in regard to the sights and ammunition for the extreme distances over which I
knew the competitions would lead me on
the morrow.

It was under these circumstances that I

went into the match the next morning, the
first stage being two hundred, five hundred
and six hundred yards. A glance at the
record will show that my first attempt here,
resulted in the respectable score of ninety-
one. This, indeed, is a very good figure,
but upon attempting the longer ranges
with different ammunition, heavier bullets
and more powder being required, laboring
also under the disadvantage which I discovered *afterward*, that the rear sight of
the rifle, instead of rising from the barrel
in a perpendicular position, inclined to the
right at an angle of several degrees; and
it was no wonder that I should, in the series
of misses that followed, hit the left wing of
the target next on the right of the one I
was aiming at.

The competitions following so closely,
one each day, left no time for me to go in
town and procure different ammunition or
to re-arrange and plumb the sights, as it
required all the evening to load the cartridges for the next day's shooting. I was
thus forced to remain at Creedmoor and

try to overcome the difficulty in the sights and ammunition with what limited means I could extemporize.

On the last day but one of the competitions the Secretary of the Association, who was still deeply interested in my success, asked permission to obtain for me another rifle with perfected ammunition and desired that I should use it the next day through the match. This I did and made the respectable total of one hundred and eighty-five. I used it also in two subsequent matches, and had the three totals been made during the days of the first competitions, it would have placed me in fourth position upon the team.

Notwithstanding this fact, the decision of those in charge of the final selection was, that Farrow must now be placed with the "*has beens*," any place on the team for him was out of the question ; they were ready to declare that, outside of the two hundred yards range, there was no one of those already nominated that could not hold his own, even with the champion of two continents.

Many were the letters of condolence and inquiry that were received after my return to Newport, to all of which I unhesitatingly answered, I could yet shoot and they should see it verified.

When the time for the Fall matches of the National Rifle Association came round, our little Newport Rifle Club were quite ready with their off-hand team, and repaired to Creedmoor, where, but for the too liberal allowance provided in the programme for the fine guns of the English marksmen, it would have taken first prize in the competition which we came there to win. Each team of four, from the British Association, was allowed six points, to be added to its total score, from the fact of its rifles being finished outside in military semblance, and having six pounds trigger pull.

The individual match, in which I expected to meet some sharp competition, and had determined to win, if possible, was the Military Champions; if I won this from all comers it would seem to be a vindication of my ability yet as a marksman. The distances were the same as those over which the competitions for team places were contested, and the last stage at eight hundred, nine hundred and one thousand yards decided the championship. A valuable gold medal and twenty-five dollars in cash were to be awarded the winner.

The value and extent of the prizes offered in this match were of such a nature, that a spirited competition was assured among the Americans, occurring as it did after the match with the British; it would be an additional honor to any guardsman or member of the team who should win this valuable trophy.

Not intending to be handicapped in any way by a defective rifle or ammunition, and wishing also to test the qualities of the rifles with which the visitors were armed, I asked McVittie, of the British team, the loan of his rifle, to use in the second stage of this match; having favored him in like manner at the two hundred yards, a few days previous, I felt no hesitation in asking.

The result of the contest was a complete vindication of my shooting abilities; I won the match with a total of eighty-five, leading the next best competitor with a margin of nine points.

"Farrow can still shoot," was passed round, and "why was he left off of the team?" And inquiries and suggestions without number were forthcoming; suffice it to say that having spent five years in the study of rifles and rifle shooting, the old saying may apply here, as "one swallow does not make summer," so, one poor score is not an assurance there is no ability in the marksman.

NOTE BY EDITOR.—Mr. Farrow now holds the medal which he won at Creedmoor, as the Champion Military Marksman of the United States of America. and is ever ready to defend his title, and prove his skill to be all that the medal implies.

Won at
800–900–1000 yards, with military rifle.
Score 85.

This photograph, contributed by Herb Peck, Jr., of Nashville, Tennessee, did not appear in the original edition of this book. The date of the photograph is unknown.

HINTS TO BEGINNERS.

Chapter I.

In these "hints to beginners," Mr. Farrow has endeavored to embody certain principles and practical suggestions in a conversational style, which we think is fully as instructive and more easily comprehended by the beginner, than any elaborate and theoretical method, however well written.—[Ed.

Tyro.—Mr. Farrow, I have determined to take up rifle shooting and give some time and attention to it; do you think it a healthful recreation?

Mr. Farrow.—Most certainly; the exercise in the open air stimulates the muscles, their training in harmony with nerve and eye, is a great relief to any strain occasioned by mental exertion and must exert a healthful reaction. What part of the art do you propose to learn?

Q.—Which would you advise?

A.—By all means the off-hand or two hundred yards shooting; if you can become proficient in this branch, your advancement to the longer ranges will be easy and more rapid.

Q.—Why! do you think it easier to make good scores at long ranges than at two hundred yards, off-hand?

A.—I do really think it far easier to become an expert marksman at eight hundred, nine hundred and one thousand yards than at the shorter distance; in the former, the position allowed the marksman is such, that after some practice, the rifle can be held as steadily on the bull's eye, as though fired from an artificial rest, and it is easier to become expert in estimating the varying forces of the wind and changes of light, which are the principal difficulties encountered at these distances.

It is easier to do that, I will say, than where a marksman is standing in the open, with no rest for his rifle but his own strength of arm and nerve, to maintain a steady hold upon the bull's eye, bringing the pressure on the trigger with sufficient force, to cause the discharge at the right instant, and following this in successive shots to the fulfillment of a complete score. Ah! yes, I could name you many who, with the experience of one season at the long ranges, have become so proficient, that scores with but few points off from the "possible," have been repeated many times, yet these same gentlemen, after years of practice at the two hundred yards, had become only medium in proficiency.

Q.—I am but a beginner in this business and am asking you some questions that would appear foolish to an old hand; now, what is meant by "32," "38" and "40 calibre?"

A.—Those figures refer to the diameter of the bore of the rifle in hundredths of an inch.

Q.—In choosing a rifle for off-hand work entirely, what calibre would you think preferable?

A.—I have found the 38 calibre the best for fine shooting at off-hand; it is the smallest calibre to which paper patch bullets have been adapted.

Q.—What are "paper patch" bullets, and are they more accurate than other bullets?

A.—Bullets that are patched have a wrapping of paper around them, to prevent the lead of which they are composed touching the inside of the rifle barrel in their passage through the tube; they are elongated bullets with a bearing inside the barrel of nearly two-thirds their entire length, and this style of bullet, where cleaning after each discharge is allowed, has been found to be more accurate than bullets with grooves in them, which must be lubricated with tallow or other material, to prevent the lead adhering to the barrel as it comes in actual contact with the rifling.

Q.—Why do you prefer the 38 calibre, can you not make as good scores with the 40?

A.—All my best off-hand work has been accomplished with the 38 calibre. I tried the 40, thoroughly, and found with the same weight of bullet, powder and rifle, more recoil in the 40 calibre than in the 38.

This question of recoil for off-hand work is very important; there is an instinctive flinching of every marksman to meet this recoil, and the lighter the "kick" of the piece the less inclination we have to meet it. The two rifles, if placed on an artificial rest, might make targets of equal excellence, but my experience is that the gun of smaller calibre and less recoil, will be far more pleasant to the shooter and give him better results for his pains.

Q.—Have you experimented with the 32 calibre, and what do you think of that?

A.—I have given some little time to the trial of the 32 calibre, but as there are no shells manufactured for this size, with a capacity for forty grains of powder, which I think is as little as we can use and maintain the velocity necessary for fine work, and also, no bullets of proper weight, shape and length could be found, I was forced to abandon the 32. The results I obtained, however, led me to view this calibre with much respect, and I am not positive that we shall not soon have even a 32 calibre, that will make excellent targets at two hundred yards.

Q.—What calibre is most generally used for the long ranges?

A.—The 45 calibre seems to be the favorite with all the manufacturers. I think the reason for this may be traced to the fact, that the government has adopted the 45 calibre for its service arm, and the manufacturers, having to prepare tools for that calibre, *forced*, as it were, the riflemen into this size for their long range work. I am of the opinion that as fine targets can be made with the 40 calibre at one thousand yards as the 45, but proper adaptation of bullet, powder and rifling, must be accomplished; and when one-half of the experiments have been carried on with this size, that there has been with the 45, we shall attain a greater degree of proficiency, and a greater degree of accuracy than is generally conceded to this calibre, and if its real capabilities were known, it would be but a short time before the government ammunition would be 40 instead of 45.

Q.—I would like to try that thing myself; could I procure a 40 calibre long range rifle?

A.—You could procure a rifle of 40 calibre that would shoot one thousand yards, but my advice would be to leave it to older and more experienced marksmen to cypher out, and begin your work at the two hundred yards, off-hand; this will tell you, after some diligent practice and study, what your capabilities are.

Q.—How would you advise a man to begin his practice for the off-hand?

CHAPTER II.

If you are aspiring to attain the highest excellence in off-hand work, a first class rifle is indispensable; it must be supplied with the bullets best fitted to its calibre, and with shells, powder and primers *ad libitum*. The manner of loading, re-loading and preparing the shells and bullets will be found a study in itself; but I do not advise you to go to the two hundred yards range and begin practicing "off-hand," that is, in the standing position; it would be better to spend at least two or three weeks shooting from a rest at the Creedmoor target.

Q.—Why! a man ought to make all bull's eyes at two hundred yards from a rest?

A.—Quite so, provided his rifle and ammunition are all right, but as a beginner, he would find that one-third bull's eyes at the start would be a very good score.

Q.—Why do you advise a beginner to practice shooting from a rest?

A.—It accustoms one to the noise of the explosion and kick of the rifle; one learns, also, after a little practice, that no bull's eye will answer his shot where the sights are not properly held, even from the rest.

Q.—You speak as though it was a difficult thing to hold the sights on the bull's eye, even with a rest.

A.—I think it a difficult thing to make a long series of bull's eyes with any rifle, and in any position; you will find when you come to try, that the noise of the discharge and the recoil of the rifle, especially if you use a large calibre, will develop in you an instinctive desire to "brace up" and meet the recoil, even though shooting with a rest.   I have found myself, when pulling the trigger at rest shooting, if I had a misfire of the cartridge, a movement of the muscles of the arm and shoulder, a tightening, as it were to brace themselves, for the accustomed kick.

Q.—Is the recoil of a rifle a very severe thing to endure?

A.—The smaller calibres in the off-hand

position are not severe in any measure, but the 45 calibre with seventy grains of powder, a beginner would consider hard punishment.

Q.—What rifle do you consider the best for off-hand shooting?

A.—There are a number of first class make of rifles, but I have learned that it is necessary, in order to develop the highest capabilities of any rifleman, that he should have an arm that would "fit" him, if I may use the expression, the conformation of the man has something to do with this; you will see marksmen with long necks and low shoulders, others quite the reverse. some with long arms and high shoulders; and I claim that each should be supplied with a rifle to suit such conformation that they can stand and "hold" in a perfectly natural position, that there may be no over strain of any series or sets of muscles, to cause an unnecessary vibration of the rifle while taking aim.

Q.—How would the rifles differ from each other to suit the different individuals?

A.—The difference would mainly be in the length and drop of the stock; the marksmen with short necks and high shoulders would require a much straighter stock and a trifle shorter; it would be quite the reverse with the long-necked and low-shouldered individual. Please bear in mind this fact, that our aim must be uniformity in everything; you must have it in the cartridge, in the sighting, in the pulling, in the position and in the holding.

Q.—What do you mean by uniformity in holding, what is that?

A.—I consider it a very important point; for instance we will take this Springfield rifle here, I will put it high up on my shoulder, the lower point of the butt-plate barely touching the shoulder; if I pull in that position, you will find the bullet to strike the target at a different point than if held in *this* position, with the butt low down and solidly braced against the shoulder, although the rifle is aimed exactly at the same point.

Q.—How do you account for that?

A.—The answer to your question would require a number of pages if the detail is gone into, but to illustrate, you will see by examining this rifle that the resistance to the recoil is below the line of fire, which is a straight line brought directly back through the barrel of the rifle over the stock; the centre of the butt-plate is about four and one-half inches below this line; now force directly back the barrel and resist on the centre of the butt; if the power applied be of sufficient strength it will cause an upward bend of the rifle, something as you would bend an opened hoop when pressing the ends towards the centre. Thus you can see if the recoil is resisted at a lower point on the butt-plate the bending up must be necessarily greater, and the nearer you can get the resistance into a straight line behind the rifle barrel, the less the bending up takes place.

Q.—How can uniformity be studied in this direction?

A.—By having what is known in the market as "Farrow's butt-plate" on the stock of your gun; this is a modification of the Swiss butt-plate, in shape and weight, to adapt it to the ten pound rifles, which only are allowed at Creedmoor. This butt you will find to clasp the shoulder, one point extending above and the other underneath; it can always be held in the same position.

Q.—I am afraid I am tiring you considerably, I will think over what you have said and call in another day.

Chapter III.

Good morning, Mr. Farrow, I have been studying over your points and would like a little more information upon the subject.

A.—Have you bought a rifle?

Q.—Hardly, after your lecture. I was at a loss which make of rifle to purchase. Going from one manufacturer to another, I discovered a new point which we had not discussed; one maker told me that *his* action only was free from any chance of accidental discharge, another told me the "safety notch" in their guns was of such perfect construction that it was impossible to have an accidental discharge with it, so "when doctors disagree who shall decide?" What do you think of the actions in the market, is there a perfect one?

A.—To this question I must answer no. I do not think there is yet offered in the market a perfect rifle action.

Q.—I am greatly surprised at that, why are they not perfect?

A.—It would be impossible to answer your question without going into details and illustrating with each particular make; but I will say this, the majority of them are too heavy, taking away from the weight of the barrel in their construction, metal, that would be of far more service and in better position to lessen the recoil and ensure greater accuracy.

The shape of certain guns is very much against them, as mentioned before, about a very crooked stock; I think they are an abomination.

Q.—Do you think a heavy barrel an advantage?

A.—I do think it an advantage, especially in off-hand shooting.

Q.—Where is the advantage?

A.—The point is right here: we will take this very Springfield rifle and you stand in position to shoot at the bull's eye; you have a pull of six pounds to release the scear; now if that rifle barrel weighs seven pounds, in the effort to make the final pull on the trigger, you will move the barrel a less distance from the bull's eye in the pulling, than you will if the barrel weighs but four pounds. Do you see the line of reasoning?

Q.—I see that you imply it is easier to pull four pounds in a given direction than it is seven; this I must admit. Are there any actions in the market with a barrel that weighs seven pounds?

A.—There are actions with barrels of seven pounds, but such rifles would not be allowed at Creedmoor because of their over weight; rifles there must not weigh over ten pounds.

Q.—Knowing all this, Mr. Farrow, I should think you would get out an action yourself, as undoubtedly you could find manufacturers to construct rifles upon your principles.

A.—I have been studying on the subject of a perfect breech action for some time, but an ingenious friend of mine named Brown, who has often exchanged ideas with me on this subject, has at last accomplished something which is the nearest to perfection in the way of breech mechanism and barrel, of anything that I have ever seen or heard of.

Q.—Where are they manufactured, and are they in the market yet?

A.—The rifles will probably be made in New York city, but are not yet in the market; dealers will have them for sale another season; but you must not put off your practice until then, though you *are* determined to have the best rifle Americans can produce. I would advise you to buy, borrow, or hire a rifle and practice with that.

Q.—What are the features necessary for a perfect breech action?

A.—First we must have a breech-block sliding at right angles with the bore of the barrel; this must have strength and solidity to withstand the heaviest of charges; the hammer may be concealed or not, but a central blow is imperative; the trigger should be so arranged that the most effective pull, is in the direction which will release its point with the minimum amount of force.

Q.—I do not quite comprehend your ideas in regard to the pull of the trigger.

A.—The sporting rifles at Creedmoor to be allowed in matches, must be able to lift a three pound weight, when attached to the trigger, without releasing the hammer. The ordinary construction of the trigger on American made rifles is such that a weight suspended in a direct line with the centre of the butt-plate, is supposed to be pulling in a direction to release the trigger with the least amount of force. Now, as I stand up with this Springfield rifle in position to shoot, you will see that the pressure of the finger on the trigger does not come in the direction of that line just illustrated, it has a more upward direction; this is one of the most important features to constitute a perfect action.

Q.—Well, good day, Mr. Farrow, you have given me much to think about; I will call again.

CHAPTER IV.

Q.—Well, Mr. Farrow, I have bought a rifle that will answer me until I find the perfect action that you mentioned, and have come to you for instruction; where does the first lesson begin?

A.—Let me look at your purchase; thirty-eight calibre, central fire shell, adapted to the patch bullet, that is correct. Now, the sights; you must have a "peep" sight and also a wind gauge for the front sight.

Q.—Wind gauge! and is it necessary to have a wind gauge? I fancied the wind would not have much influence upon a bullet going two hundred yards What is the use of the wind gauge anyhow?

A.—You will believe me, after some practice, that the best plan is to always hold with the sights at one particular spot on the target; if you have no wind gauge it is impossible to comply with this: one day the wind will be from the left, carrying the bullet three or four inches to the right of the zero point on the target, the next day the wind may be from the right, which would blow the bullet as much in the opposite direction; this would keep you aiming first on one side of the bull's eye and then on the other, while with the wind gauge you make corrections for this drifting of the bullet with the wind and always hold at the same point.

Q.—How do you make these corrections on the wind gauge for the drifting of the bullet?

A.—The wind gauge is a sliding sight with a zero point; it is adjustable with a screw. The sliding part is in the shape of a thimble, containing the pin-head or aperture sight with which we draw our aim. I always use what is called the pin-head sight, and in aiming place on the target immediately under the bull's eye at six o'clock.

Q.—What do you mean by "six o'clock under the bull's eye?"

A.—It is a part of rifle nomenclature to use an imaginary watch dial, not only on the target, but also on the range. In the former, placing the dial inside the bull's eye, a shot striking on the centre upper edge, would be a " twelve o'clock bull; " one at the bottom edge would be a " six o'clock bull," and so round for the different figures. On the range the six o'clock point of the dial represents the shooter, the twelve o'clock the target, and the wind blowing from the direction of the figures is denoted as a wind from that quarter; for instance, a nine o'clock wind would be from left to right, directly across the range; a three o'clock would be exactly in the opposite direction.

Q.—Why do you always hold the sight at " six o'clock " under the bull's eye; why not hold the pin-head *on* the bull's eye.

A.—In holding the pin-head on the bull's eye, I found it was impossible, sometimes, to tell whether it was *on* or *above* the bull's eye, and have often been credited with " twelve o'clock fours," or " centres," as they call them at Creedmoor, when I was certainly sure of a perfect pull with the sight *on* the bull's eye. This happened so frequently that I at once changed the point of aim, and must say it was a great improvement.

Q.—Now will you explain to me how to use this wind gauge?

A.—I will set our wind gauge on the zero point; if we shoot with a perfect aim and the bullet lands on the target at good elevation, but outside of the bull's eye to the left, we will then understand that the wind has drifted the projectile four or five inches in that direction. To make the proper corrections it will be necessary to move our wind gauge in the same direction from its zero point that the bullet has taken on the target; as the point with which we draw our line of sight is in the thimble and moves with the wind gauge, you will perceive that in the moving, the muzzle of the rifle is carried against the wind; our next bullet will go into the wind and then swing back for the centre of the bull. We thus divide, with the second bullet, the distance which our first one was forced away from the central line of the target.

Q.—You spoke of aperture sights; what is the aperture sight and do you never use it?

A.—I only use the aperture disc for long range work; there you will find it very useful; it is a small circle of steel in which the bull's eye must be properly centred to obtain good results. I have discarded it for off-hand work, having found on a windy day it was almost impossible to use it with success.

Q.—What is this little glass attachment here?

A.—There, hold the rifle *so*, you will perceive a little bubble; this is a spirit level with which to detect any deviation of the sight from a true perpendicular; we can detect with it the slightest twist of the rifle in either direction. I only use it for the longer ranges.

Q.—What do these marks and figures indicate upon the bar of the peep sight?

A.—They are arbitrary divisions, and being numbered, facilitate the using of the vernier scale to correct the elevations in hundredths of an inch. After once locating your elevation for two hundred yards, you will seldom have to change more than a point or two with the same ammunition.

Q.—This hole in the peep appears very small; I can scarcely see through it, and objects have a *fuzzy* appearance.

A.—Let me look at it. It is far too small, and the fuzzy appearance you describe is occasioned by too much metal; there is a diffraction of light inside this tiny little peep hole. You will find nearly all factory-made sights in this same condition. We must run a drill with an oval shaped point into the peep disc towards the eye, cutting out the metal and only leave a very thin edge to surround the peep hole; then we get a clearer and better view of the target and front sight. This is a very important point, many marksmen thinking that the finer the peep hole the more accurate will be their aim, but they make a mistake, the eye will naturally seek the *centre* of the hole in the peep, as the view at that point is clearer and more distinct, and after a little practice you will detect instinctively any wandering of the eye from this position.

Q.—Now that I understand the use of the peep and wind gauge, what practice had I best begin?

A.—I cannot commend too highly to you the importance of what I call "home practice," that is, placing upon the wall or lamp shade a tiny bull's eye, one eighth of an inch for ten feet distance is about the size, then assuming the position as if in actual contest, aiming at the bull's eye and snapping the rifle, of course without any cartridge in, at the tiny point. This will educate your finger and eye for real work, and must be learned quite thoroughly before you may ever expect to become a prize winner.

Q.—How long should I practice at this?

A.—Half an hour twice a day. Morning and evening would be a good time for training. This practice will appear to you rather monotonous and something like taking medicine, but it is as important as the latter and fully as efficacious.

Q.—How long must I practice this before going to the two hundred yards at a rest?

A.—At least one week's time ; your finger and eye will then become partially educated and you will be able to fire a few shots without so much of that involuntary "bracing up," which is the bane of "off-hand" riflemen.

You will find in your first practice hard work to prevent the eye from closing when the hammer strikes. When you are positive you can snap ten shots without winking, it will be time for you to try the two hundred yards at rest.

Q.—Well, good day, Mr. Farrow, I intend to follow out your directions and will give it a thorough trial.

Chapter V.

Tyro.—Here I am back once more, Mr. Farrow.

Mr. F.—Good morning, I am very glad to see you, indeed I had nearly given up seeing you again; let me see, it is some two weeks since you were here.

Q.—Yes, sir, I found the task you set me more difficult than I expected, and I determined to bother you no further until I had accomplished the feat satisfactorily.

A.—I am gratified to find you so painstaking, it is the only sure road to success. Let me see how well you can go through the trial.   Here! aim at this spot.

Q.—Shall I snap the hammer?

A.—Certainly, I want to see the exact mode of practice you have been taking. Is that the way you have been holding your rifle?

Q.—Why! yes, this is the position I saw the riflemen in pictures, and supposed it was the correct attitude to cultivate. What is your position for two hundred yards off-hand?

A.—I do not wonder you devoted two weeks' time before you accomplished what you desired, if practicing with the left arm so, fully extended under the barrel. In learning the use of the shot gun, I would advise the left arm extended, but not too fully so; in your two weeks' practice you have undoubtedly discovered that the longer you supported the rifle, the greater the vibration and trembling, the point of support being so far from the body, increasing as the continued strain is sustained.

Q.—I have detected all that you say, and would like to cultivate the proper and most successful style of holding.

A.—There are a number of modifications of the style of holding which I advise. My own position, you will see, is natural and easy. I place the butt of the rifle against my shoulder *thus*, the muzzle resting upon the table in front. Now, then, I place the thumb of the left hand under the trigger-guard, the fingers fully extended and touching the fore-end of the rifle stock in such a way that a sort of cradle is formed of the first three fingers, making an elastic cushion of the finger tips, which is a most desirable plan .in the way of a rest for the rifle. I now lift the muzzle of the rifle up to the line of the target; my left elbow is pressed against the side of the body, and if your conformation is such that it will touch the hip, so much the better, it gives you a more perfect rest with which to support the weight of the rifle barrel; you will perceive the vibration or trembling of the weapon is reduced to the minimum, and in your practice now you will also find less of that circular and sweeping motion, but a gentle side motion, which depends a great deal upon the movement of the body Now, the position of your feet will help you to overcome this swinging motion; stand evenly and firmly upon both feet with toes well turned out, the left side nearly in line with the target; this will bring your chin in position so that it rests upon the check-piece of the stock; it is a great help, it steadies the head and prevents the eye from wandering around the aperture in the peep sight.

Q.—I found great difficulty, in the position in which I practiced, to retain through the peep a clear view of the bull's eye, my head having a trembling or vibratory motion. Let me try your position now. [He takes the gun, puts it up and tries to get the position; the elbow does *not* rest upon the hip; it is the case with many riflemen.]

A.—There, that is about the thing, but your conformation is such that your elbow does not reach the hip and I would advise a modification of this position; rest the trigger-guard upon the palm of the hand, the fingers still extended under the fore-end; swing the elbow well across the chest and draw it tight in; you will thus form nearly as solid and as perfect a rest as in the other.

Q.—I perceive at once the advantages in favor of your method and would have

called to see you before if I had been practicing in this position.

A.—Now let me see you snap the rifle.
[He takes it up and is in the act of taking
aim.] One moment, your finger is hardly
on the trigger. Have you been practicing
pulling with the first joint only?

Q.—Why! certainly, I have had no
instructions in that way and presumed it
would be proper.

A.—You must press the trigger with the
centre part of the second joint of the finger,
placing it well around in a hooked position,
there, so. The trigger, we will presume,
pulls off at three and a quarter pounds
pressure; now put two pounds or as much
as is possible upon the trigger without
releasing the scear. After practice in
" holding," the rifle will come for an instant
to a dead stop, that is, the instant in which to
apply the extra pressure and cause the discharge; the rifle will frequently settle, but
at a wrong point; you must command your
finger pressure to such a degree as to
restrain it from a pull at such a moment.

Q.—I think I quite comprehend your ideas, Mr. Farrow, and tomorrow I shall take my first shoot at two hundred yards. You still advise me to begin from a rest?

A.—By all means, I would advise you to devote at least two or three days of each week for some time, shooting from a rest at two hundred yards on a Creedmoor target. Let me know how you succeed tomorrow, I am somewhat interested in your success.

Chapter VI.

The pupil appears crestfallen; his scores were not up to the mark he had expected.

A.—Well, sir, here you are again, just returned from your practice; now what success?

Q.—Well, Mr. Farrow, I don't know, hardly, what to say; I fancy this gun is nearly worthless.

A.—You haven't had the success you anticipated in your rest shooting?

Q.—By no means, my first few shots seemed to follow with some regularity, but I soon lost the bull's eye, and in fact, missed the target in a number of instances.

A.—I am not greatly surprised at that, it being your first experience. How was your ammunition loaded?

Q.—Ammunition? It was some that I purchased already made; it came direct from the factory, or at least, I was so assured. Do you think the ammunition could be in fault?

A.—I have never yet seen factory ammunition that could be relied upon for that accuracy necessary in target shooting at two hundred yards. How did you treat the rifle barrel, did you clean it after each shot?

Q.—Why, no, I didn't clean it from the very start.

A.—You have yet a great deal to learn after you have mastered the difficulties of holding and the art of pulling the trigger at the right instant; you have yet an interesting study in the treatment of the inside of the rifle barrel and the preparation of your ammunition.

Q.—Do you prepare your own ammunition?

A.—Most certainly, I would hardly trust any one to load cartridges for me. The kind and quantity of powder used, the cleaning of the shells, the proper seating of the primer, the material of which the wad is composed, are all necessary and vital points of which I must be well assured.

Q.—Do you think these points you have mentioned are of so much importance?

What effect does the seating of the primer have upon the accuracy of the bullet?

A.—You will remember my caution to you about studying uniformity in everything. You must remember it in the priming of your shells as well as other points. Suppose we have a primer settled firmly to its seat in the shell; the blow from the hammer will cause the flash from the primer to permeate the powder charge to a certain depth; we have another primer partially settled, not firm in its seat, the same blow from the hammer will force the primer *down* and will give a less forcible explosion, the flash entering the charge of powder to less extent than before; the combustion of the powder is influenced by these two forces, the one developing a greater instantaneous combustion and a larger quantity of gas before the bullet escapes from the muzzle than the other, consequently, producing a flatter trajectory and showing a difference on the target between the two cartridges of from six to eight inches.

Q.—Your argument is truly a forcible one, I must admit; I would like to prepare some cartridges under your direction. How do you reload your shells?

A.—The shells should be properly cleaned and carefully dried and the primers seated well down. I am satisfied to measure, not *weigh* the powder, and load each shell through a tube of at least twenty-four inches in length. This gives the powder a fall of sufficient force to pack itself in the shell with greater uniformity and less trouble than by shaking or tapping it; then place a ward, cut from thin card board or stout blotting paper, to retain the powder in its position. If there is a shoulder in the chamber, at the muzzle of the shell and base of the rifling, I do not consider it the better way to seat the bullet in the shell, but drop it into the chamber of the rifle and push it with a stick or instrument made for the purpose, up into the rifling until the base of the bullet is in front of the shoulder; then insert the loaded shell.

I am presuming you are using the *paper*

patch bullet, as we know it will give the best results.

Q.—Did you say I must clean the rifle after each shot?

A.—Most assuredly. You would think a *clean* barrel should give better results than one full of powder dirt and *debris* from the cartridge. There are brushes with rubber attachment to facilitate the cleaning. The brush is wet with water and simply pushed through the barrel with a cleaning rod, then followed with one rag; this will be sufficient to ensure good results on ordinary occasions.

Q.—I will again say good day, Mr. Farrow, you have given me renewed confidence in this rifle, and my next attempt shall not fail from lack of good ammunition.

A.—I am very much interested in your success; as soon as you have made your ten consecutive bull's eyes at two hundred yards from a rest, if you will call again, we will take a trip to Creedmoor together. If possible, it shall be on the day of a match. I will see how you go through the ordeal.

Chapter VII.

By appointment *Mr. Farrow* meets *Tyro* at the Ferry on the way to Creedmoor.

Q.—Mr. Farrow, I have been waiting for you some time.

A.—I am very glad to see you so early on the ground; it is really a vital point to be early at the range if you desire to become a winner of the first prize; there is always an anxious or slightly nervous feeling experienced by every marksman that enters a match and really strives for the first position; by being a little in advance of your brother riflemen this feeling has time to get worn off, and will affect you less when your turn comes to shoot.

Q.—You are always ready with some "point," I see; I wonder what will be the next one?

A.—I wish to make a prediction; that notwithstanding all the points I have given you I shall find that you have been experimenting with your ammunition already.

Q.—Why! what makes you think so?

A.—My whole experience has been that way. I have started a great many riflemen and shown them my exact methods; in a very short time I have found them experimenting in all sorts of ways, and I fancied you would be no exception to the rule. Of the entire number that I have helped on the way, I can remember but one that implicitly followed my instructions without any variation or experiments. He shot well from the start, soon was a prize winner, and made it very interesting for me in many matches.

But here we are on the other side. Have you joined the Association?

Q.—No; this is my first visit to Creedmoor, and I had not thought of it.

A.—The Railroad trains do not run direct to Creedmoor; you must get tickets for Queen's and go by stage from there to the range.

Q.—How awkward that is; I fancied

the trains landed us directly at the firing
points.

A.—Far from it ; but you will see enough
to interest you while on the way. There
is a number of other marksmen in the car ;
before we return you shall make their
acquaintance.

Q.—Do you think they are all going
into the match?

A.—Undoubtedly the majority of them
will take part. And here is another
" point : " don't let your mind dwell on *how
many competitors* there are, *who* they are,
or *what their record*—strive to think of
something entirely disconnected with what
you are about to do. This anticipation of
events has broken up many a sure winner.
If, in the beginning of your experience,
you cultivate that folly of watching your
competitors, seeing what they are doing,
minding their scores instead of attending
entirely to your own affairs, or get thinking of what somebody else is doing, how
many bull's eyes this one or that one is
making,—you will surely go the way of

the ordinary marksman. You must, if possible, eliminate from your mind all ideas of what the other competitors are doing; give your whole attention to making a bull's eye of each individual shot.

Q.—That will come rather hard with me as I am always curious to know what my neighbors are doing.

A.—That is generally the way, especially with beginners. It takes a great deal of nerve to cultivate this restraint, but by all means do make the effort. Halloo! here we are at Queen's Station; I wonder if we shall get a seat in the wagon. It is quite interesting, the way those gentlemen are running and scrambling for their seats, but take it cool, take it quiet. Let us arrive there as free from excitement as possible.

Q.—Do we ride far?

A.—The carriage takes us to the Club House on the Range, where we will make the entries for the match and then walk to the firing points. I think we will be in time to hire a target for half an hour and get some practice before the match begins.

It will give an opportunity to correct our elevations and windage. Many a match has been lost by starting with a wrong elevation or without proper allowance for the wind.

Q.—This is the Club House, I presume. Creedmoor is really a beautiful place. What are those long, low targets in the distance? [Supposed to be looking from the Club House, down the range.]

A.—The targets you see are six feet high by twelve feet wide, and are used at the extreme distances. Let us go down to the two hundred yards firing point; I see the superintendent is there; we will have some practice. Is this your first attempt at off-hand, two hundred yards?

Q.—I have shot a few times while out at rest-shooting, but never a complete score.

A.—Were you quite successful in shooting from a rest?

Q.—Oh! yes, I made the ten Creedmoor bull's eyes some time ago. I have lately been practicing on the ring target.

A.—You will find your elevation for off-hand somewhat higher than for your rest shooting; place it at five minutes or hundredths above and try a shot. You will also find it is more difficult "*holding*" here at Creedmoor than any other range, being completely unsheltered from the breeze makes it very trying, especially on a windy day. Many fine marksmen have been disappointed at Creedmoor, not being able to attain the same scores at two hundred yards they make so easily at their own ranges.

Q.—Here come the marksmen; we must close our practice. Shall I shoot on the same target with you?

A.—I presume not. The squadding is usually done by "drawing for targets." Please remember now my instructions about being indifferent to your neighbors' movements, watch only your own score; see to it that the score-keeper puts down the proper figure after each shot. Many a match has been lost by a mistake of the score-keeper in not putting down the correct figures.

[*Mr. Farrow* interviews the Secretary and returns with the score cards.]

You are squadded on Target No. 7, while I am on Target No. 2. We will meet again at the conclusion of the match.

[Mr. F. wins the contest with a score of forty-seven. The pupil has actually made a score of forty-two with two "magpies;" this gives him four bull's eyes in the ten shots.]

How have you enjoyed your first experience?

Q.—I hardly know; I really tried to follow your instructions to the letter. I felt inclined, though, to blame the marker at the target for one or two shots I expected bull's eyes for. What do *you* think of my first attempt?

A.—Let me see your score ticket. How did you finish your string? Three—four—three! Looks rather suspicious on the end. I think you must have become a trifle nervous.

Q.—You are quite right. I was well satisfied and doing nicely until two or three marksmen from the other target came up and examined the scores; perforce I had

to follow their lead and became so anxious
over my succeeding shots that I nervously
flinched, pulled them away from the bull's
eye.

A.—Your first experience is undoubtedly
a valuable one.   Let us go back to the one
thousand yards firing point and see what
the Long Range shooters are doing.   You
should be well satisfied with this first
attempt, and if you will carefully continue
your home practice and remember the
"points" that I have tried to inculcate, you
will certainly succeed.

In conclusion I wish to impress one more
"point" on your mind.   If you ever lose
confidence in your gun, ammunition, or
ability, go at once to the two hundred yards
range and shoot from a rest, upon a paper
target; there you will at once discover which
is at fault.   A first class rifle will put ten
consecutive bullets in a four inch circle at
two hundred yards.   Don't satisfy yourself
with off-hand practice in a case of this kind.

Q.—I will do my best to follow your
instructions.

A.—Have you ever seen any long range practice? If not you will be somewhat surprised at the position which some of the shooters assume.

Q.—Which do you consider the strongest position?

A.—The "back position;" it is most generally adopted now. The shooter lies partly upon the right side, the left hand grasping the rifle barrel in front of the action. The peep-sight is carried as near to the end of the butt stock as possible, because the greater the distance between the sights of the rifle, the more accurately can the elevations be adjusted. The left foot is planted firmly upon the ground, with the knee in a nearly perpendicular position, the right leg clasping the left ankle, thus forming a V shaped rest, and one in which the pulsations of the body influence the rifle the least. The butt-plate rests firmly against the shoulder, while the right hand grasps the stock in such a position that the first finger rests upon the trigger. A number of shooters bring the left hand to a position immediately in front of the peep-sight, and have a short leather strap attached to the left wrist; this is seized by the teeth and makes a very convenient support for the head and neck.

Q.—What a loud noise those guns make? What calibre are the rifles?

A.—They are forty-five calibre, and use from one hundred to one hundred and fifteen grains of powder with five hundred and fifty grains of lead. The recoil from these guns is very near two hundred pounds at each discharge. The regulations allow the use of pads and cushions to prevent the marksman from getting bruised.

Q.—How about preparing this amunition?

A.—My remarks on preparing ammunition for the short range, will apply as well for the long range; also as to the manner of cleaning the rifle; it must be done after each discharge. Great difficulty is experienced by long range riflemen in getting bullets of precisely the same diameter and density of material. This will explain, in a great measure, why a marksman to-day makes a most brilliant score, and another day, when another batch of bullets is used, his scores fall far below the average. But lately, an instrument called a " sizer" through which the bullets are pressed to give them a uniform diameter, is generally used by the most experienced marksmen.

Q.—What rifle is best for this distance ?

A.—There is not much choice between the different makes of rifles in the market, but whichever one you choose, don't fail to shoot it at the two hundred yards, and unless you can shoot ten bullets so that a four inch circle will contain them, there is some defect either in ammunition, gun or holding.

Q.—How do you detect the variations in the force of the wind ?

A.—This is only to be done by what can be discovered from the flags that are posted on the range. Creedmoor is very poorly flagged, having few flags and those situated on but one side of the range. The shooters that are squadded on the extreme right hand targets have a great advantage over those in the middle of the range, and the majority of the high scores recorded at Creedmoor were made upon these right hand targets.

This long range shooting is another branch of study of the art; each particular rifle will require some peculiar management or treatment almost entirely different from its neighbor, due to the fitting of the shell, or the depth of the rifling, or kind of primers, the kind of powder, or thickness of the patches, the care in cleaning necessary to ensure uniformity in the inside of the barrel, all these, and many other points will require careful attention.

Q.—Your experience at Creedmoor would be very valuable to a beginner, and if I ever take up long range work, I shall surely need your assistance.

Mr. Farrow.—Good bye, Mr. Tyro, any points upon which you are in doubt or need information, even news of that "perfect breech action," I will most cheerfully give, a letter sent to Newport, R. I., will surely find me.

Friends :-

The writer has endeavored to give in these pages his personal experiences in becoming proficient in the art of rifle shooting. Much has been written on the subject, theories advanced, lines laid down with rules for practice, etc., all of which possess more or less merit; the author commends them to the attention of inquiring minds and simply tells his story. If any inaccuracies should seem to appear to those friends familiar with these scenes, I would remind them that they were seen but through mine *own* eyes. I have not the gift that Burns craved,

> " Oh ! wad some goodie the giftie give us,
> To see oursel's as others see us."

W. MILTON FARROW

After a great deal of persuasion, amounting almost to persecution on our part, we assisted in the preparation and induced Mr. Farrow to publish this interesting narrative. As this is our first attempt to assume the duties of editorship, any faults of omission or commission we trust will be judged leniently.

EDITOR.